D0526369

A Way with Words

Vocabulary development activities
for learners of English

Book 3

Stuart Redman

Advisory editor: Michael McCarthy

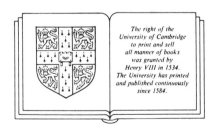

The right of the
University of Cambridge
to print and sell
all manner of books
was granted by
Henry VIII in 1534.
The University has printed
and published continuously
since 1584.

INSTITUTE FOR APPLIED LANGUAGE STUDIES
UNIVERSITY OF EDINBURGH
21 Hill Place
Edinburgh EH8 9DP

Cambridge University Press
Cambridge
New York   Port Chester
Melbourne   Sydney

Published by the Press Syndicate of the University of Cambridge
The Pitt Building, Trumpington Street, Cambridge CB2 1RP
40 West 20th Street, New York, NY 10011–4211, USA
10 Stamford Road, Oakleigh, Victoria 3166, Australia

© Cambridge University Press 1991

First published 1991

Printed in Great Britain at the University Press, Cambridge

ISBN 0 521 35921 X Student's Book
ISBN 0 521 35922 8 Teacher's Book
ISBN 0 521 35028 X Cassette

Copyright
The law allows a reader to make a single copy of part of a book
for purposes of private study. It does not allow the copying of
entire books or the making of multiple copies of extracts. Written
permission for any such copying must always be obtained from the
publisher in advance.

GO

Contents

Thanks

Rob Ellis, my co-author on Books 1 & 2, has continued to provide me with ideas and support, as has Ruth Gairns, who has been a rich source of ideas and inspiration throughout the last three years.

In many respects, Jeanne McCarten and Michael McCarthy have been the backbone to this project. Without their wit, wisdom and endeavour, it would not have been possible.

Chitose Sato and Petrina Cliff, for giving permission to use their source material.

The many schools and colleges throughout the world who were kind enough to pilot the material and provide such invaluable feedback.

And finally, thanks to Lindsay White and the rest of the production team at CUP.

Acknowledgements

The author and publishers are grateful to the following authors, publishers and others who have given permission for the use of copyright material identified in the text. While every effort has been made it has not been possible to identify the sources of all the material used and in such cases the publishers would welcome information from copyright holders.

HarperCollins Publishers for the extracts from *Collins COBUILD Essential English Dictionary* on pp. 4 and 88; Chronicle Features, San Francisco, California, USA for permission to reprint *The Far Side* cartoons by Gary Larson on pp. 10, 12, 61, 68 and 100; *EFL Gazette* for the text on p. 13; *Sunday Mirror* for the article on p. 21; Royal Mail for the postal delivery photograph on p. 21; Penguin Books Ltd for the table from *Living With Stress* by Cary L Cooper, Rachael D Cooper, Lynn H Eaker (Penguin Books, 1988), © Cary Cooper, Rachael Cooper and Lynn Eaker, 1988 on p. 29; Times Newspapers Ltd and Tim Rayment for the article © Times Newspapers Ltd 1985 on p. 30; Andrew Mann Ltd for the ALEX cartoon on p. 31; J Allen Cash Photo Library for the photographs on pp. 37 and 102–3; Piste Artistes for the adapted text and photographs on pp. 38–9; Rogers, Coleridge and White Ltd, Literary Agency for permission to reproduce the adapted extract from *The Book of Heroic Failures* by Stephen Pile on p. 40; *Punch* for the cartoons on pp. 45 and 90; Guardian News Service Ltd for the articles on p. 46 and the cartoon on p. 91; *The Mail on Sunday* for the article on p. 47; Express Newspapers plc for the article 'Ambulance Chaos set to worsen' on p. 56; *The Independent* for the article 'Ambulance staff step up pay action' on p. 56; *She* for b), d) and e) on p. 57; *The Sporting Life* for c) on p. 57; *Ms London* for the article on p. 59; Editors Press Service, Inc for *The Far Side* cartoons by Gary Larson on pp. 62 and 99; NSP Group Ltd for the photographs and text from *The Innovations Report* on pp. 72, 73 and 124; Evening Standard Company Ltd for the article on p. 78; *The Observer* for the adapted text on pp. 102–3; *Private Eye* for the cartoon by Nick Newman on p. 108.

Drawings by Chris Evans, Lisa Hall, Leslie Marshall and Shaun Williams. Artwork by Peter Ducker, Hardlines and Wenham Arts.
Book designed by Peter Ducker MSTD.

1 Learning

1 Keeping vocabulary records

a The page below is taken from a student's vocabulary notebook. With a partner, write down the different techniques the student has used to record and remember new words and phrases.

Example:
Writing down a translation for a new word.

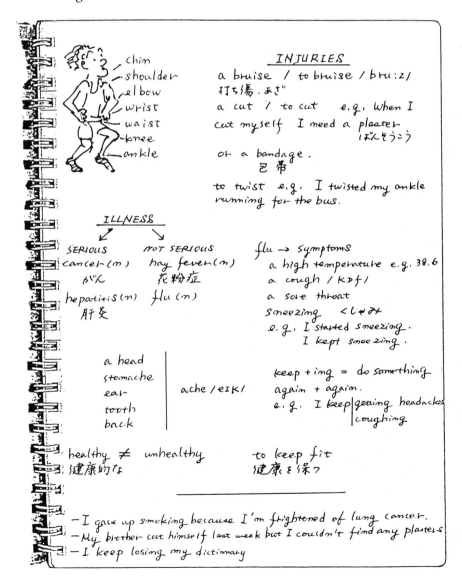

b Now look at a page from your own vocabulary notebook. Is it very different? Are there any techniques from this page that you think would help in the future?

—— 2 Word grammar ——————————

a It is not enough just to know the meaning of words – you must also know the grammar of vocabulary otherwise you will make a lot of mistakes in speaking and writing.

Example:

It depends ̶o̶f̶ you. (*depend* is followed by the preposition *on*)

Can you find a word from the box which is being described in each of the sentences below?

avoid	weather	pick up	purchase	go out
fond	guess	quid	desert	win	tell	keen

1 It's an uncountable noun.
2 It's a word which is usually used in formal situations, and is more common in written English than spoken English.
3 It's a transitive verb so it must be followed by an object.
4 It's a verb which is followed by a gerund (an *–ing* form).
5 It's an adjective which is followed by the preposition *of*.
6 It's a separable phrasal verb.
7 It can be a verb or a noun, and as a verb it is irregular.
8 It's a very informal (colloquial) word so normally it is only used in spoken English.

b In the following letter there are a number of mistakes. Correct the mistakes and then explain to a partner why you have made these changes.

```
                          c/ San Fernando 239
                          Cordoba
                          14003
                          Spain

Dear Sir,
      I would like an information about English courses at
your school in July and August.
      I studied English for six years at school and in my
job I read many books and articles in English so I am
quite good in understanding the language. My problem is
speaking because I don't have any opportunities to
practise so I need a course to brush up it. I enjoy to
study but I only have one month so I would like a course
very intensive - perhaps five or six hours a day.
```

A friend recommended your school and also said me
that you arrange accommodation. It would be a great
pleasure for me stay with an English family but I would
like to live near the school, if possible.

If you need more information you can drop me a line
at my home address or my work address.

I remain,
Yours faithfully

Juan Rodriquez

——— 3 Taking risks with vocabulary ———

a If you only offer the minimum amount of information when you speak in
English, your active vocabulary will not improve very quickly because you
are not creating opportunities to use and learn new words. So don't take the
easy way – take a few risks. For example, read the following text about an
accident a woman had in her car, and then try to answer the questions
below.

I had an accident yesterday when I was driving home from work. A car
came out of a side road and hit the side of my car. I wasn't hurt
fortunately, but my car was quite badly damaged. It was terrible.

1 What speed were the cars doing?
2 Why did the other car pull out of the side road?
3 Did the woman see the other car before it hit her?
4 How did she react when it hit her?
5 How did the other driver react? What did he do?
6 Was anyone else involved?
7 Was anyone injured?
8 Did the other driver admit it was his fault?
9 What damage was there to the cars?
10 Were there any other witnesses?
11 Did anyone contact the police?
12 Was the woman able to drive the car home?

b With a partner, rewrite and expand the story so that a reader could
answer all of the questions above.

c Give your story to another pair and see if they can answer all of the
questions.

—— 4 Using dictionaries ——

a Some verbs are very important because they are used in many different situations and with different meanings.

Example:
  I keep making the same mistake. (*keep* = do it again and again)
  They kept me in prison. (*keep* = make someone stay)

Look at the six sentences below showing different meanings of *leave*. Write the translation for *leave* for each of these sentences and then compare your answers with someone who speaks the same language.

	Translation	*Definition number*
1 The train leaves in ten minutes.	abfahren (German) salir (Spanish)	
2 I'm afraid I left my books at home.		
3 I left the company last year.		
4 I've only got £10 left.		
5 She left her husband two years ago.		
6 You can leave your coats here.		

b Now look at the dictionary definitions below. In the right-hand column above, write the definition number which corresponds to each of your sentences.

leave /liːv/, **leaves, leaving, left**. **1** If you **leave** a place or person, you go away from that place or person. EG *My plan now was to leave for the seaside... My train leaves Euston at 11.30... They left the house to go for a walk after tea... He stood up to leave... I left Conrad and joined the Count at his table.* **2** If you leave a place or institution, you go away permanently from that place or no longer attend that institution. EG *Many of the children I met had left home after a savage beating... What do you want to do when you leave school?... She told him she was going to leave her job and move to London... All they want to do is leave at 16 and get a job.* ◊ **leaving** EG *...a leaving present.* **3** If you **leave** someone that you have had a close relationship with, for example your husband or wife, you stop living with them or you finish the relationship. EG *Look, you mustn't tell Henry I'm leaving him... My husband had left me for another woman.* **4** If you **leave** someone or something in a particular place, you let them remain there when you go away. EG *Leaving Rita in a bar, I made for the town library... I left my pack behind and took only my water bottle... If you leave things on the floor, they get trodden on.*

V OR V+O
⇑ depart

V OR V+O
⇑ quit

◊ ADJ CLASSIF :
ATTRIB

V OR V+O
⇑ desert
= abandon

V+O+A

5 If you **leave** something somewhere, **5.1** you forget to take it with you when you go away from a place. EG *I had left my raincoat in the restaurant... Millie had left her watch behind.* **5.2** you put it where someone can find it and use it or you put it where it will be safe while you are away. EG *Leave your phone number with the secretary... Castle left his bicycle with the ticket collector at Berkhamsted station.* **6** If you **leave** someone doing something or **leave** them to an activity, you allow them to carry on with what they are doing when you go away from them. EG *We left him snoring in the front room... He left them making their calculations... I left her to her knitting.* **7** If you **leave** someone to himself or to herself, you go away from them so that they are alone. **8** If you **leave** a certain amount of something or if something is **left**, it remains when the rest has been taken away or used. EG *Nine from sixteen leaves seven... He drained what was left of his drink... Leave some of the stew for the boys... There was only about ten minutes left of the lecture.* ● If you **have** something **left**, you have it after the rest has gone or been taken away or used. EG *I only had two pounds left... How many pills have you got left?...*

V+O+A

V+O, V+O+O, OR
V+O+A (for/ with)

V+O+-ING, OR V
+O+A

V+O+A (to)+O
(REFL)

V+O

● PHR : FIRST VB
INFLECTS

c Write six questions which could produce different meanings of *leave* in the answer. Can your partner answer using the verb *leave*?

SELF-STUDY ACTIVITIES

1 Most of the time we do not remember words if we only see them once. It is therefore very important to revise new vocabulary. One simple way is to leave space at the bottom of each page in your notebook and then return to this space one week later and write down three or four sentences using some of the words from the page. You can see an example of this in the page from the student notebook in exercise **1**. Try it yourself over the next month and see if it helps you to remember words from previous lessons.

2 Using some of the ideas for recording vocabulary from exercise **1** of this unit, organize the words and phrases below in a more helpful and memorable way. You can add more words of your own, but remember to leave some space at the bottom of the page to add sentences of your own in the future. Compare your page with a partner's in the next lesson.

match	win	professional	fit	aerobics	serve
agile	draw	volleyball	gym	practise	train
game	clumsy	athletic	squash	badminton	amateur
beat	unfit	tennis	set	lose	get (a bit of / a lot of) exercise
play (a game)	sweat	basketball			

3 Write two sentences for each of the following verbs, showing them being used with different meanings. Check your answers in a dictionary and add any other meanings you think are useful.

catch   miss   mean   manage   lose   break

2 Putting things in order

—— 1 ——

a Adjective word order is very complicated but the columns below show a typical order for describing people and clothes.

Opinion	Size	Shape	Colour	Material	+ Noun
lovely ugly	big tall	round fat	grey	cotton	

Put the following words into the correct column above:

leather	thin	square	blond	long	scruffy
broad	greenish	gold	cashmere	suede	filthy
nylon	fair	pointed	huge	dark	steel	pale
tiny	short	smart	muscular	bright (+ colour)

There are exceptions to this order. Adjectives describing opinion can sometimes be placed after those describing size, shape, or even colour, but this is not always possible.

Example:
scruffy, long black hair ✓ or long, black scruffy hair ✓
a lovely, long grey dress ✓ but not a long, grey lovely dress ✗

b Complete the following story with adjectives from above.

The woman was able to give the police a detailed description of her attackers. One of the men was tall and .... with short .... hair, ... skin, and .... blue eyes. He was wearing a .... grey suit with a .... blue .... jumper underneath, and he had an expensive-looking .... ring on the index finger of his left hand. In contrast, the other man was much shorter, but with .... shoulders and a very .... build. He also had short hair but it was .... and quite curly, and his face was .... than the other man's with a .... chin. His clothes were old and .... He wore blue jeans, an old black .... jacket, and a pair of .... red trainers.

c Describe different people in your class and see how quickly a partner can guess who you are talking about.

—— 2 ——————————————

a Rewrite the sentences below using the adverbs in the box to replace the underlined words. The meaning must stay the same.

generally	invariably	hardly ever	repeatedly	occasionally
barely	regularly	partly	probably	definitely	often

Example: *often*
            I don't see her a ~~great deal~~ nowadays.
                  ^

1 She eats meat <u>about twice a year</u>.
2 I agree with you <u>to a certain extent</u>.
3 Our receptionists are female, <u>almost without exception</u>.
4 <u>As a rule</u> she does her job very efficiently.
5 I've told him <u>a hundred times</u> to keep his keys in a safe place.
6 <u>Once in a while</u> he loses his temper.
7 I think there's <u>a very good chance that</u> she'll get the job.
8 I could walk <u>about three steps</u> when I came out of hospital.
9 She'll pass the exam <u>without a doubt</u>.
10 I visit my parents <u>twice a week</u>.

b   Compare your answers with a partner. What position do these adverbs go in, and how many of them can go in more than one place in the sentences above?

c   Using the adverbs above, modify the following sentences so they are true of yourself. Then compare your sentences in groups and discuss them.

1 I use a dictionary when I'm studying English at home.
2 I repeat words to myself in English.
3 I talk to myself in English.
4 After lessons I revise new vocabulary at home.
5 When I forget words I feel it's my own fault.
6 I can remember new vocabulary from the previous lesson.

---— **3** ——————————————————————————————————

a Put the words on the right into the correct place on each line of the story.

The doctor's car drew up at eight o'clock.	outside
'The patient slept soundly,' I said. 'In fact, she is alseep now.'	still
He didn't look at me, but instead walked straight through	even
to the sickroom and examined her. It took a long time, for	quite
despite his efforts, she didn't wake up fully.	still
'Is she getting protein in her diet?' he asked.	enough
'She eats solid food,' I replied.	hardly ever
He scribbled a prescription on a grubby form, closed his bag	carelessly
and left. For some reason I felt relieved and when I told my	greatly
father-in-law I was going to get some medicine, he breathed	also
a sigh of relief and we smiled. 'She'll soon be better,' he	both
said.	

b Compare your answers with a partner and check them with your teacher.

c Now continue the story, putting the words into the correct place.

I decided to take Leela with me on this occasion. I had	hardly ever
time to take her out these days and she looked thrilled.	enough
Her little friend was playing when we left. Leela said,	outside
'Can Sami come, please?' The two girls were very alike and	as well
when we got to the shops they chose the same sweets. It	even
was a warm day and I let them play on the swings on the	quite
way back.	
When we came to the corner of the street they were excited	still
from their game. Immediately I saw the doctor's car outside	almost
the house and I told the children to go and play. They scampered	both
off giggling. Fortunately they hadn't noticed the car, but in	even
any case, they were not old enough to understand.	yet

d Compare your answers with a partner and try to form your own rules for the use of these words.

e With your partner, write the last part of the story. Try and use several of the words above.

—— **4** ——————————

a **Put the words in the list into the correct columns below.**

former   forthcoming   ex-   current   next
ancestor   predecessor   last   latest   successor
previous   recent   descendant   late

Past	Present	Future

b **Using these words, complete the following sentences. There may be more than one possible answer.**

1 Can you name two .... holders of the World Cup (football)? Do you know who the .... holders are?
2 Who is the .... secretary of the United Nations and who was his/her ....?
3 Can you name a possible .... to the United States as the richest country in the world?
4 Spielberg's .... film is about the war. I don't like it as much as his .... film.
5 What do you think our .... would have thought of our way of life?
6 And what do you think our .... will think of it?
7 She had been a widow for three years, but a day never passed without her thinking of her .... husband.
8 The political parties believe the .... election in June will be a very close battle.
9 The President was accompanied by the .... President and political leaders from a number of European countries.
10 What do you think will be the .... major change in the world of technology?

SELF-STUDY ACTIVITIES

1 Ordering words along a scale can also help you to remember the meaning of different words, for example:

   freezing→cold→lukewarm→warm→hot→boiling (for water)

Put the following groups of words along a scale and add any others you know which might also go on the same scale. (One word or phrase in each group appeared in the story in exercise **3**.)

a) giggling   grinning   roaring with laughter
b) for a while   for ages   for a split second
c) thrilled   satisfied   pleased
d) wrote   printed   scribbled
e) drew up   pulled up sharply   screeched to a halt
f) scampered   sprinted   jogged

2 Look up the meaning of the following adverbs (if necessary), and then decide which ones could be used in the sentences below. Can the adverbs go in more than one position in the sentences, and if so, does this change the meaning of the sentence?

| foolishly   bravely   accidentally |
| deliberately   reluctantly   willingly |

a) The documents were thrown away.
b) I answered all his questions.
c) She tried to save the drowning child.
d) When he pulled out a knife I got out of his way.
e) He spent the whole day in bed.

3 Character and personality

a Most people know certain quotations, often funny or clever, which describe a type of person or human quality. Can you match the quotations below with the correct word on the right?

1 Doing the right thing without being told.
2 Someone who believes everything is beautiful, including what is ugly.
3 One who knows the way but can't drive the car.
4 Knowledge of cowardice in the enemy.
5 One who, when he has the choice of two evils, chooses both.
6 The inner voice which warns us someone may be looking.
7 A person we know well enough to borrow from, but not well enough to lend to.
8 The bigger a man's head, the worse his headache.
9 A person who talks when you want them to listen.
10 A man who knows the price of everything and the value of nothing.

a) a pessimist
b) bravery
c) conceit
d) an optimist
e) conscience
f) a bore (a boring person)
g) initiative
h) a cynic
i) a critic
j) an acquaintance

b Discuss the quotations in groups. Which ones do you find . . .

1 the most amusing?
2 the most cynical?
3 the most accurate?
4 the most difficult to understand?

c Do you know any similar quotations or proverbs in your own language which you can translate into English?

——— 2 ———

a The statements below were made by three different people. With a partner, decide which four statements were made by each person. There is one statement per person in each group of sentences.

1 I was never very good at school but I always tried to do my best.
2 I rarely did homework when I was at school.
3 I did very well at school and I always knew I would be successful.

4 I should make more effort to get a job but I'm not bothered about a career.
5 I was so nervous that I made lots of mistakes in my first job.
6 I can't afford to make mistakes in my job, and I never make excuses if I do.

7 If you want to be successful, you're bound to make enemies.
8 I always make an effort to be nice to people.
9 I can't stand people who make a fuss about punctuality.

10 I find it difficult to make friends.
11 I prefer to let other people make decisions.
12 I believe in speaking my mind. It doesn't do any good hiding your feelings.

b Choose three adjectives from the list below which best describe each of your three characters. Discuss your answers in groups.

lazy   shy   self-confident   arrogant   vague   dynamic
modest   ambitious   ruthless   weak   easy-going
frank   boring   practical   selfish   honest   unreliable

c All of the sentences in **a** above contain expressions with *do* or *make*. How many can you remember without looking at the sentences? Write them down and then compare your answers with a partner.

d ⌧ You will hear one of the characters from **a** talking about their home life. Which character is it, and why? Can you also write down five expressions with *do* or *make* that the person uses?

'And another thing . . .
I want you to be more
assertive! I'm tired of
everyone calling you
Alexander the Pretty-
Good!'

—— 3 ——

a What is the difference between being a translator and an interpreter? In groups, decide if the qualities below are necessary for translators, for interpreters, or for both. Use a dictionary to help you.

excellent pronunciation   a very wide vocabulary   methodical
a fluent speaker   creative   the ability to summarize quickly
flexible   a knowledge of colloquial language   academic
outgoing   thorough   intuitive   quick-witted   patient
a good memory   articulate   youngish (i.e. under forty)

b An English professor studied these two jobs, and the text below describes his conclusions. Do they confirm or contradict your own ideas?

The results refined some traditional stereotypes: one that translators were introspective, bookish, painstakingly slow but thorough and correct in the use of written words, and made use of long-term memories, whereas interpreters were outgoing and eloquent, had to show empathy towards other people, were quick, intuitive and approximate, and thus made use of short-term memory strategies; another that interpreting is predominantly a young woman's occupation, while translating concerns all ages, including over 50-year-old starters, with many transfers coming from a multitude of other professions.

The author explains that the two activities cannot be compared, since both present different approaches to treating language and problem-solving: the translator has to apply perseverance and patience, consult subject specialists and sleep on the problem until it is resolved. By contrast, the interpreter, living on his/her wits, is required to perform a sudden reflex reaction and provide the first reasonable answer that comes to mind, like a summary or a paraphrase, otherwise ignore the difficulty and carry on.

Ultimately, Henderson found no evidence as to which factors are of major importance when recruiting potential future professional linguists. A too perfectionist translator would be low in productivity and not very cost-effective; a glib extrovert interpreter could not work effectively in a team.

c Notice how the words below are used in the text to contrast the two different subjects. Using these words, write sentences of your own contrasting journalists and novelists.

whereas   while   by contrast

SELF-STUDY ACTIVITIES

1 How many words can you build using the nouns from exercise **1a** and the
   adjectives from exercise **2b**? You can check your answers using the
   word-building tables at the back of the book.

General noun	Personal noun	Adjective	Verb
cynicism	a cynic	cynical	————
reliability	————	(un) reliable	to rely (on)

2 Choose a job and then make a list of the qualities and skills normally
   associated with it (look at exercises **2b** and **3b** for examples). In your next
   lesson, read your list to a partner and see if they can identify the job.

3 Think of ways in which your own personality has changed in recent years,
   and write them down.

   Example:

   I've become more self-confident.
   I've become less idealistic.

Use a dictionary to help you, and then compare your answers with a friend in
the next lesson. Do they agree with you?

4 Nouns

—— 1 ——

a Nouns in English can be countable, uncountable, or both:

Countable	Uncountable
a lovely day	lovely weather (not a lovely weather)
cars are dangerous	knowledge is dangerous (not knowledges are)
there's a hair in my soup	he's got blond hair (not blond hairs)

Making the minimum of changes, rewrite the sentences below using the words on the right. Most of the words are uncountable, but not all of them, so be careful.

Example:
   What a beautiful day.   weather

   What beautiful weather.

1	Have you got many suitcases?	luggage
2	The pasta is ready.	spaghetti
3	The latest reports from China are disturbing.	news
4	She owns a few small firms.	company
5	You can put the table and chairs over there.	furniture
6	Are there any places left on the bus?	room
7	I sent the parcels this morning.	package
8	Did you have any problems getting here?	trouble
9	There are lots of drawbacks.	disadvantage
10	You can get the details from reception.	information
11	I asked the teacher to advise me.	advice
12	How many years have you had as a journalist?	experience

b How many of the uncountable nouns can also be used as countable nouns? Use a dictionary to find out and then write sentences to show how they can be used as countable nouns.

—— 2 ——

a When we combine two nouns we can use -'s on the first noun, or link the nouns with a preposition:

1 The -'s is often used with personal names and nouns, animals, countries, collective nouns, and temporal nouns. For example: Peter's dictionary, the committee's report, a week's holiday.

2 A preposition is more common with inanimate nouns. For example: the title of the book, the end of the film, the purpose of the visit.

Combine nouns from the two boxes with either -'s or *of*.

tower   Beethoven   cat
government   hour   facts
Britain   envelope   Mary
nephew   knife   water

bike   summary   fifth symphony
responsibility   balance of payments
paw   blade   height   surface
back   jewellery   delay

Example:
Mary's jewellery; the surface of the water

b Now write a short story using the nouns in the list below. Combine the nouns using the two constructions above. You can use a noun more than once, and you can combine a noun with different nouns if you wish.

garden   branch   bottom
neighbour   Fred   shoulder
ladder   roof   Betty   shed
top   cage   kitchen   tree

c Listen to the woman telling the same story and write down any combinations she uses which do not appear in your own story.

—— **3** ——

a With time expressions we can also make the first noun an adjective. For example, three weeks' holiday *or* a three-week holiday.

The second construction is common with expressions of measurement, and in each case the adjective becomes singular and hyphenated. For example: a ten-minute walk, a three-month-old baby, a six-inch ruler.

b Complete the following sentences with a suitable expression.

1 We had a ....-............ delay at the airport.
2 The prize went to a ................-............-............ child from Oxford.
3 It's a ....-............ hotel so it will be expensive.
4 We've just been on a ....-............ cruise in the Mediterranean.
5 It's about a ....-............ drive to my mother's house.
6 You'll have to climb a ....-............ fence to get in.
7 You can measure the water with that ....-............ jug.
8 The new car has a ....-............ engine so it's more powerful.
9 I'm not very hungry so I don't think I could manage a ....-............ lunch.
10 The newspaper is offering a ................-............-............ reward for information leading to the arrest of the murderer.

c One problem with English measurements is that they are different from those of most countries. Can you answer the following questions? The table below will help you.

1 Which is longer, a two-mile walk or a three-kilometre walk?
2 Which is higher, a six-foot fence or a two-metre fence?
3 Which is longer, a twelve-inch ruler or a thirty-centimetre ruler?
4 Which holds more, a one-gallon can of petrol or a four-litre can of petrol?
5 Which holds more, a two-pint jug or a one-litre jug?
6 Which is heavier, a ten-pound bag of sand or a four-kilo bag of sand?

Weights and measures		
Linear measure		
	1 inch	= 2.54 cm
12 inches	= 1 foot............	= 0.305 m
3 feet...............	= 1 yard...........	= 0.914 m
1760 yards.......	= 1 mile...........	= 1.609 km
Capacity measure		
	1 pint............	= 0.568 litres
8 pints.............	= 1 gallon	= 4.54 litres
	1 US gallon	= 3.78 litres
Weight		
	1 ounce	= 28.35 g
16 ounces	= 1 pound........	= 0.454 kg
14 pounds........	= 1 stone	= 6.35 kg

—— **4** ——————————————————

a   Two words often combine to form a new word. For example: income tax, teacup, traffic jam, earthquake, day trip, bookcase.

These words are called compounds. Sometimes they are written as one word and sometimes as two words. Hyphens are sometimes used but this is usually with compound adjectives. For example: easy-going, broad-shouldered.

Find eighteen compounds in the list below using the words provided, while your partner goes on to **4b**.

writing *paper*	.... card	black ....
post	head	hand ....
back	paper	.... office
.... board	.... market	.... box
pocket	tooth	pick ....
.... ache	money	.... phone(s)

b   How many compounds can you find in the following picture?

C   **Exchange answers with your partner and see if you can add any more words in a or b.**

---

1 Use a dictionary to find out whether the following nouns are countable, uncountable, or both. Write your own sentences to show how they can be used.

training   luck   dress   work
flu   travel   job   equipment

2 Choose a newspaper article or a page from a book you are reading, and see how many examples you can find of the three noun constructions you have studied in this unit. That is to say:

   – the -'s construction, e.g. my neighbour's garden;
   – the *of* construction, e.g. the end of the road;
   – compounds, e.g. headache, identity card.

3 How many different compounds or common word combinations can you create using the words in the following list?

   Example: you can have a vice-president and a vice-chairman, but not a 'vice-manager'.

leader   secretary   chairman   vice   manager   personal
personnel   assistant   president   political   deputy   party

5 Changes

—— 1 ——

a There are many verbs in English which contain the idea of change in their meaning. Underline all the examples you can find in the text below and look carefully at the way they are used. For example, do you think you could replace an underlined verb with another underlined verb? Can you find satisfactory translations for each underlined verb?

I've been to England many times but on my last visit I decided to bring my car. It was a disaster. I found it almost impossible to adapt to driving on the left with a left-hand drive car. For one thing I had to adjust all my mirrors and I still couldn't see very much; and then I discovered they had altered the one-way system in Dover since my last visit, so I kept going down streets the wrong way. In the end I decided to switch to a right-hand drive car. Fortunately I had an English friend who was going to Italy, so we swapped cars. It took me a while to get used to changing gear with my left hand, but after that it just transformed my whole attitude to driving in England – I even began to enjoy myself. Of course, these things can vary a lot from person to person: a friend of mine has driven a left-hand drive car in England for years and never had any problems.

b Now choose the correct answer or answers in the following questions.

1 It's a very useful bag because you can .... the strap.
   a) adapt   b) change   c) adjust   d) transform
2 The motor car has .... the lives of millions of people.
   a) changed   b) switched   c) transformed   d) adjusted
3 Old people sometimes find it difficult to .... to change.
   a) swap   b) switch   c) adapt   d) alter
4 We were going to visit my uncle but he is ill so we had to .... our plans.
   a) change   b) alter   c) vary   d) switch
5 We used to have an electric cooker but then we .... to gas.
   a) swapped   b) switched   c) changed   d) altered
6 The dress was lovely material but it was too big so I had to .... it a bit.
   a) transform   b) alter   c) adjust   d) vary
7 My work .... so much from week to week that I never get bored.
   a) adjusts   b) changes   c) varies   d) adapts
8 If we .... places, you'll have a much better view.
   a) change   b) adjust   c) alter   d) swap

c How will you understand and remember the differences between these words? How much do translations help you? Will explanations in your first language help? Which verbs require sentence examples? Can diagrams help you with the meaning? Work with a partner who speaks your language to make a clear record of these words.

—— 2 ——

a   How many things in the list below might disappear by the year 2000? Work with a partner and give reasons for your answers.

dentists   taps   tinned food   an all-male clergy   telephones
surgery   keys   postmen/women   glasses (spectacles)

b   Read the text below and compare the predictions with your own ideas. When you have finished, go back and complete each space with a suitable word.

GOODBYE

THE year 2000 is just around the corner, and the world we live in is about to change before our very eyes.

By the year 2000 many of the things we consider .... won't be around any more. Such as:

DENTISTS Good oral hygiene and new advanced toothpastes will .... cavities and gum disease.

TAPS Because of pollution, the water won't be fit to drink. Drinking water will come in bottles and washing up will be done by ....

DISPOSABLE NAPPIES Valeting services will return soiled nappies fresh 'n' clean within hours, so the "old fashioned" nappy will come back.

VENICE The beautiful city may disappear altogether because of pollution to its ....

TINNED FOOD People will switch to fresh, long life, natural and .... food so canned produce will disappear.

PHONES We will take to wearing tiny phones on our .... like watches. Phones as we know them will be museum pieces.

**By ALAN BURNS
Medical Editor**

SPECTACLES Space-age eye surgery may make spectacles look like something out of the Ark. Glasses could well become ....

POSTIES The fax machine will become as common as phones are today. Postmen will be rare.

VIDEO RENTAL SHOPS Families will order a video by phone that arrives in moments down fibre optic lines.

KEYS .... cards that open doors will totally replace keys.

SURGERY "Going under the knife" will lose its meaning. .... will take place by laser so there will be no need for all that blood.

ALL-MALE CLERGY Things will change as more women become ministers. Even the Vatican may allow women ....

c   The actual words used in the text are in the list below. Compare these words with your answers and consider the following questions.

essential   wipe out   dishwashers   foundations   organic
wrists   obsolete   plastic   operations   priests

1 If you had the same answers, what information in the text helped you?
2 If you had different answers, are your answers also possible in the context, and in what way are they different in meaning from the actual words used in the text?
3 If you had answers which are completely wrong, can you see why they are wrong?

d   In groups, make a list of six things which will either disappear or change significantly by the year 2000. Give your list to another group and see if they agree with you.

—— 3 ——

a   How would the following changes affect you personally? Answer the questions beginning with one of the phrases in the list below.

How would you feel if . . .

1 The price of petrol went up by 30 per cent?
2 Bus fares rose by 30 per cent?
3 The government put up the legal age to drive a car by two years?
4 The government raised the school leaving age by two years?
5 Your school said they were going to alter the timetable and start lessons one hour earlier?
6 Your teacher told you the school was moving to a new building next month, which was one mile to the north of the present building?
7 The government made it illegal for people to own more than one property?
8 Your school decided to raise its fees by 25 per cent and reduce the number of students in a class by the same amount?

   I'd be really fed up because . . .
   It would affect me quite a lot because . . .
   It wouldn't affect me very much because . . .
   It wouldn't bother me at all because . . .
   I'd be delighted because . . .

b   In groups of four try and predict what each person wrote and then find out what they actually said.

Example:
   A to B: I think it would affect you quite a lot if bus fares rose by 30 per cent because you haven't got a car.
   B to A: Well, actually it wouldn't affect me very much because I don't need to take the bus very often.

—— **4** ————————————————————————————

a 🔲 **Listen to the conversation about the changes made to a sports centre and answer the following questions.**

1 What has been covered?
2 The building has been extended. What for?
3 What has happened to the old café?
4 What have they got rid of? Why?
5 What have been swapped round, and why?
6 What has been installed in the gym?
7 What has been slightly altered? How has it been slightly altered?
8 What has been abolished?

b Of the words and phrases below, which might be used to describe the old sports centre, and which might be used to describe the new centre?

run-down   trendy   shabby   modern   posh
old-fashioned   well-equipped   unsafe   smart

—————| **SELF-STUDY ACTIVITIES** |————————————————————

1 How will the things in the sentences below change? Complete each sentence with a suitable verb from this box.

fade   cure   shrink   melt   expand   increase
dissolve   reduce   grow   heal   decline   swell

a) If you wash a woollen jumper in hot water, it will ....
b) If you take ice cream out of the freezer, it will soon ....
c) If you put sugar in hot coffee, it will ....
d) If you heat metal, it will ....
e) If you put a carpet in a sunny room, the colours will gradually ....
f) If you remove a plaster, a cut will soon ....

Can you put the remaining six verbs into correct sentences?

2 As society changes, new words are needed to describe those changes. Do you know the meaning of the following new words? Can you guess what they mean? Try and find out for your next lesson.

satellite broadcasting   passive smoking   head-hunter
football hooliganism   the greenhouse effect   yuppies
perestroika   hands-on   ageism   catalytic converter

3 Prepare notes for a short talk on something in your experience which has changed greatly, e.g. your home town. Be prepared to give your talk in the next lesson.

6 Revision and expansion

1

Complete the following sentences with a suitable verb.

1 In the match last night, Italy .... Spain 3–1.
2 Italy .... 3–1.
3 The price of petrol has .... from 45p to 48p a litre.
4 The oil companies have .... the price of petrol from 45p to 48p.
5 Interest rates have .... from nine and a half to nine per cent.
6 The government has .... interest rates from nine and a half to nine per cent.
7 He .... me he was going to be late.
8 He .... he was going to be late.
9 Could you .... how this works?
10 Could you .... me how this works?

2

A number of English words are commonly shortened, e.g. *telephone* usually becomes *phone*. What is the short form for each of the following?

influenza   gymnasium   veterinary surgeon
sales representative   mathematics   bicycle   refrigerator
laboratory   advertisement   personal computer ·

3

Complete the following phrases in a logical way.

1 The title of the ....
2 The blade of the ....
3 A bag of ....
4 Verdi's ....
5 Picasso's ....
6 The vet's ....
7 A twelve-inch ....
8 A ten-pound ....
9 The branch of the ....
10 A summary of the ....
11 A tube of ....
12 Beethoven's ....
13 Shakespeare's ....
14 An hour's ....
15 A six-foot ....
16 The edge of the ....

— 4

Complete the crossword below with common phrases and compounds.

Across	Down
1 tooth...............	1 pick...............
4 tea...............	2 .... throat
6 .... Eve	3 ....-going
8 income	4 .... disc
9 .... tennis	5 ....box
12 five-............... hotel	7 .... market
13 writing	10 back...............
14 washing-...............	11 day ....
	12 ....-in-law

— 5

a Find the odd man out in each of the following groups of words. The answers are all connected with pronunciation.

1 bruise   cruise   ruin   suit   fruit
2 leather   heal   sweat   healthy   spread
3 author   thorough   ruthless   thin   bother
4 hay   pale   vary   vague   phrase
5 honest   hour   huge   knee   knowledge

b 🔲 Now listen to the tape and check your answers.

— 6

Which three adjectives in the list below are the most important qualities for a successful politician? Discuss your answer in groups.

frank   ruthless   eloquent   conceited   thorough   creative
flexible   quick-witted   methodical   honest   dishonest
dynamic   outgoing   practical   selfish   good-looking

— 7 —

Write questions which could produce the following answers, and then read each of your questions to a partner to see if they can give the logical reply.

1   No, hardly ever.
2   No, I gave it up last year.
3   No, it wouldn't bother me at all.
4   No, she didn't even offer me a drink.
5   Yes, but I much prefer her latest.
6   No, he's the former leader.
7   No, I'm afraid not. I can give you some plasters, though.
8   Yeah, I'm afraid there's a nasty dent in the boot.
9   I'm afraid it shrank.
10 No, no problems at all. I followed the map, and it's quite well signposted.

— 8 —

Write a description of the accident shown in the picture below, and then compare your story with a partner's. Working together, can you improve both stories?

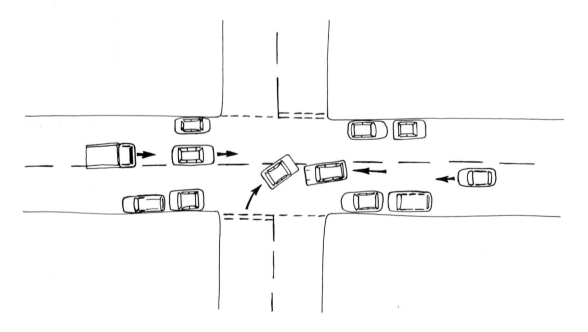

—— 9 ——

Find a synonym or antonym for each of the words in this list, then read your words to a partner. Can they give you the correct synonym or antonym from the list?

conceited   deliberate   hurt   shy   get rid of
successor   quid   trendy   purchase   foolish   huge
rare   reluctant   fond (of)   bravery   essential   fluent
extrovert   posh   as a rule   without a doubt   once in a while
to a certain extent   barely

—— 10 ——

a   Decide whether the underlined letter in each of the following words is pronounced /ɪ/ as in *sit* or /aɪ/ as in *side*, and then put the words in the correct column on the right.

	/ɪ/	/aɪ/
reliable symptoms hepatitis pint shy prejudice wrist dynamic cynic tiny agile promise wipe out symphony		

b   Now listen to the tape and check your answers.

—— 11 ——

Write down something:

1 that can melt
2 that can dissolve
3 that can fade
4 that can expand
5 that can decline
6 that can vary

7 you can abolish
8 you can alter
9 you can adjust
10 you can swap
11 you can extend
12 you can't avoid

12

---

a Look back at the vocabulary records you have kept since you started using this book. Have you used any of the techniques you saw in Unit 1 for storing vocabulary? If so, do you think they are helping you? If not, is there a particular reason why you haven't used them? Discuss your answers in small groups.

b Here is another idea for vocabulary storage which can also help you to revise vocabulary. Look at the vocabulary you have learned in two different exercises, and then try to combine it. The underlined words in the following example all appeared in exercises **2** and **4** of Unit 5.

Dental Hospital

PROBLEMS	SOLUTIONS
building is run-down	do repairs and paint it
foundations are unsafe	strengthen foundations
interior is shabby	decorate it and put in some plants and pictures
equipment is obsolete	install new equipment
long queues for essential surgery	employ more dental surgeons
theatre for operations is tiny	extend it
cloakrooms unhygienic:	
— water not fit to drink	provide bottled water
— towels quickly get dirty	switch to disposable paper towels
furniture in reception is old	get rid of it and buy new furniture
system for appointments inefficient	alter it
old-fashioned image	advertising campaign to create smarter image

---

7 Work

--- **1** ---

a Some jobs are more stressful than others. Consider the following five jobs and decide which is the most stressful and which is the least stressful. Work in groups.

banker   librarian   miner   teacher   politician

b Now look at the stress league below compiled by a national newspaper. Are you surprised at the results?

THE SUNDAY TIMES

Your place in the stress league

Rating is from 10 to zero: the higher the rate the greater the pressure

Miner	8.3	Farmer	4.8
Police	7.7	Armed forces	4.7
Construction worker	7.5	Vet	4.5
Journalist	7.5	Civil Servant	4.4
Pilot (civil)	7.5	Accountant	4.3
Prison officer	7.5	Engineer	4.3
Advertising	7.3	Estate Agent	4.3
Dentist	7.3	Hairdresser	4.3
Actor	7.2	Local government officer	4.3
Politician	7.0	Secretary	4.3
Doctor	6.8	Solicitor	4.3
Taxman	6.8	Artist, designer	4.2
Film producer	6.5	Architect	4.0
Nurse, midwife	6.5	Chiropodist	4.0
Fireman	6.3	Optician	4.0
Musician	6.3	Planner	4.0
Teacher	6.2	Postman	4.0
Personnel	6.0	Statistician	4.0
Social worker	6.0	Lab technician	3.8
Manager (commerce)	5.8	Banker	3.7
Marketing/export	5.8	Computing	3.7
Press officer	5.8	Occupational therapist	3.7
Professional footballer	5.8	Linguist	3.7
Salesman, shop assistant	5.7	Beauty therapist	3.5
Stockbroker	5.5	Vicar	3.5
Bus driver	5.4	Astronomer	3.4
Psychologist	5.2	Nursery nurse	3.3
Publishing	5.0	Museum worker	2.8
Diplomat	4.8	Librarian	2.0

Source: University of Manchester Institute of Science and Technology

—— **2** ——

a What are the causes and effects of stress at work? With a partner, complete the boxes below with possible answers.

Effects on health

```
1
2
3
4
```

Causes of stress

```
1
2
3
4
```

Stress

Effects on companies

```
1
2
3
4
```

b Now read the text and check your answers. Add any information from the text which you have not already included in your network.

Working can be a health hazard

by Tim Rayment

As concern spreads about Britain's continuing high rate of heart disease – Scotland has the worst rate in the world – occupational stress is coming under increasing scrutiny. The Health and Safety Executive, the EEC and researchers on both sides of the Atlantic are investigating.

The reasons for the job being considered stressful vary. One expert said last week that dentists, with a suicide rate twice the national average (stress rating 7.3), are often failed doctors who dislike being feared as inflictors of pain. Miners (rating 8.3) top the table because of the hostile environment in which they work. Pop musicians (rating 6.3) suffer financial insecurity, performance nerves, and rigorous self-criticism.

Stress at work can cause raised blood pressure and lead to heavy drinking, depression and mental illness or heart disease. It can make difficulties for organisations, too: high absenteeism and labour turnover, and poor industrial relations and quality control. Strikes, accidents and apathy are the likely results.

Cooper draws attention to three reasons why normal work pressure, which is healthy and stimulating can turn into dangerous stress:

• Lack of autonomy. The study of tax officers, which will be published later this year, reveals much dissatisfaction with the "autocratic" style of senior managers.

• A poor relationship with superiors. They – like parents – should reward as well as punish.

• The dual-career family. Husband and wife must be flexible if each is to pursue a career. Not all employers help. Some refuse to recognise that asking one person to move to another area can disrupt two people's jobs, even though 64% of women now work.

3

a Find sentences from the list on the right which paraphrase each of the sentences on the left. You will not need to use all the sentences on the right.

1 What do you do for a living?
2 Is it a very rewarding job?
3 Do you get any perks?
4 Why did they sack you?
5 Are you in charge of recruitment?
6 Is it a very demanding job?
7 What does the job involve?
8 Why did you hand in your notice?
9 How much do you earn?
10 Is it a skilled job?
11 Why did they take you on?
12 Are you freelance?

a) Why did you resign?
b) What do you have to do exactly?
c) Where do you live?
d) Do you work for yourself or are you employed by someone?
e) Why did they employ you?
f) Is it a very satisfying job?
g) Do you need any special training?
h) Are you responsible for employing people?
i) Is it very hard work?
j) What's your salary?
k) Why were you dismissed?
l) Do you get paid for overtime?
m) What's your job?
n) What fringe benefits are there?

b It is sometimes necessary to paraphrase what you are saying if the listener does not understand.

Example:

    A: How much do you earn?   C: Why did they sack you?
    B: Sorry?   D: I beg your pardon?
    A: What's your salary?   C: Why did they dismiss you?
    B: Oh, it's . . .   D: It was because of . . .

Practise similar dialogues with a partner using phrases from **a**.

c Find someone in your class with a job and interview them about their work. Choose suitable questions from **a**, and any others you want to ask.

—— **4** ——————————————————————————

a   Discuss the following three jobs and decide who would do the things in the box below most often.

a secondary school teacher
the managing director of a small company
an army sergeant

attend meetings   obey orders   negotiate contracts
mark essays   cancel appointments   shout at people
fire people   delegate work   make unpopular decisions
set a good example   appear to be in a good mood   tell lies
encourage people   complain about work   compromise
apologize   go on strike   take risks   sign documents

b   Which of the things in the box would you personally find most difficult? Discuss your answers in groups.

SELF-STUDY ACTIVITIES

1 Find out the meaning of the underlined phrases in the following sentences and be prepared to explain them to a partner in the next lesson.

   a) He has always taken his job very seriously but recently he has become a complete workaholic.

   b) They gave her a golden handshake when she left the company.

   c) I told him that I was up to my eyes in work and couldn't possibly go out with him this evening.

   d) They've just employed a new financial adviser – a real high-flier according to the people in the accounts department.

   e) He told me to pull my socks up otherwise I'd be out of a job.

   f) That Mrs Bates is a real slave driver.

2 Match words in the left-hand box with words in the right-hand box to form six compound nouns. Then use the words to complete the sentences below.

out	down	set		log	over	fall
back	turn	break		put	back	down

   a) Manufacturing .... has fallen steadily in the past five years.

   b) There's always a .... of work waiting when I get back after my holiday.

   c) The problem was caused by a complete .... in communication.

   d) The strike will be a big .... for the company.

   e) Last year .... reached almost £3 million.

   f) Trying to expand too quickly brought about their ....

3 If you have a job, try the following over the next week. Write down:

   a) the name of everything on your desk.

   b) the name of all the equipment in your office.

   c) five duties specific to your job.

   d) three major objectives of your company.

8 Prepositions and phrases

—— 1 ————————————————————

a ⊡ Listen to the interview and complete the table below.

	Man	Woman
Something you are . . . 1 fond of 2 interested in 3 afraid of 4 worried about 5 good at 6 shocked by 7 allergic to 8 looking forward to 9 thinking of doing fairly soon		

b Now move round the class and interview other students in the same way. When you have finished the class can decide which was the most unusual answer for each question.

—— 2 ————————————————————

a How many phrases can you find by combining the prepositions on the left with the words on the right?

at	in	earth	first	heart	average	all	holiday
on	by	tears	last	random	far	least	the way

b Where could you put these phrases in the following sentences? When you have finished, read your sentences to a partner and discuss the answers.

Example: _on holiday_
I think she's away ∧ at the moment.

1 There were forty people at the party.
2 How are you going to buy a Mercedes on your salary?
3 We had to stop for petrol.
4 I learnt that poem when I was at school.
5 I visit my parents twice a week.
6 It's the best record they've ever made.
7 She enjoyed the film but I didn't like it.
8 She broke down when I gave her the news.

9 The soldiers started firing into the crowd.
10 I found it quite difficult but I got used to it after a while.
11 We spent hours looking for somewhere to eat, and then we found a little
     restaurant that was open.
12 The film's about a couple who give up their jobs and expensive lifestyle in
     the city and move to an old cottage in the country where they can grow their
     own food and lead a simple life. Do you know what time it starts?

c Complete the following sentences using the above phrases. When you
have finished, get into groups and try to predict what each person has
written.

1 I spent . . .	4 I met . . .	7 She was . . .
2 I learnt . . .	5 I chose . . .	8 I didn't . . .
3 How . . .	6 I waited . . .	

—— **3** ——————————————————————————

a Complete the sentences on the left with the correct phrase from the right.

1 She introduced me . . .	a) for helping her clean up the mess.
2 She prevented me . . .	b) for the bad results.
3 She accused me . . .	c) to the attractive girl sitting in the corner.
4 She congratulated me . . .	d) from the crowd of press photographers.
5 She mistook me . . .	e) of stealing her pen.
6 She blamed me . . .	f) from joining the navy, but I took no notice of her.
7 She thanked me . . .	g) from leaving the building.
8 She reminded me . . .	h) on passing my driving test at the fifth attempt.
9 She discouraged me . . .	i) for a famous pop star.
10 She protected me . . .	j) of a close friend who'd been killed in a car crash.

b Which emotion might best describe how 'I' felt in each of the above
situations? You may wish to use some of the following adjectives:

delighted   grateful   upset   frustrated   jealous
sad   flattered   annoyed   relieved   puzzled

c Rewrite the following sentences using the above verbs.

Example:
'This is my cousin, Juliette.'

She introduced me to her cousin, Juliette.

1 Well done – I knew you'd win.
2 That's very kind of you to carry my suitcase.
3 It's your fault we lost the tickets.
4 I think you'd be a fool to accept the job.
5 I'm sorry, but no one is allowed to leave.
6 You're not telling the truth.
7 You're the Prime Minister of the UK, aren't you?
8 You look just like my niece.

—— 4 ——

a Complete the following sentences using *at, on* or *in*. If you are not sure of the answer, look at the diagrams below and see if they help you.

1 It's .... the top shelf .... the kitchen cupboard.
2 We met .... the bus stop .... Cavendish Street.
3 The office is .... the fourth floor, ... the far end of the corridor.
4 We live .... Southwold which is .... the east coast.
5 I saw it .... page seven .... the evening paper.
6 We put the picture .... the wall .... the living room.
7 He's sitting .... that table, next to the man .... the grey suit.
8 If it's not .... that map, have a look .... the big atlas.
9 I must have dropped it .... the floor when I was .... the dentist's.
10 I left school .... sixteen, spent a couple of years working .... a boat, and
    then I got a job .... London.

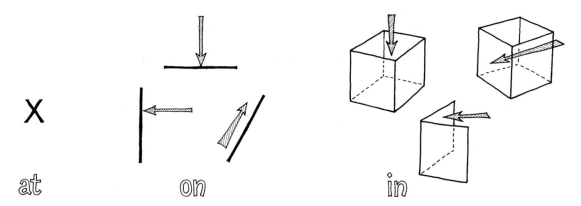

X

at   on   in

b With a partner, can you explain the difference in meaning between the following pairs of sentences?

1 a) We went on the lake.   b) We went in the lake.
2 a) We arranged to meet at the cinema.   b) We arranged to meet in the cinema.
3 a) It's at the back of the book.   b) It's on the back of the book.
4 a) We sat on the grass.   b) We sat in the grass.
5 a) It's on my way.   b) It's in my way.
6 a) It's in that magazine.   b) It's on that magazine.
7 a) She's at the office.   b) She's in the office.

SELF-STUDY ACTIVITIES

---

1 Look up the meaning of the following phrases in a dictionary and then find a
   suitable place to insert them in the sentences below.

all of a sudden	at first glance	at the time
for the time being	in the end	on the spur of the moment
from a distance	on second thoughts	

a) It was a terrible shock but I soon got over it.
b) It was a terrible journey but we got there.
c) I was tempted to dive off the cliff, but I decided it might be a bit dangerous.
d) I hadn't made any plans; I just decided to go.
e) I was driving along the motorway and then the engine just burst into flames.
f) It looked like quite a nice restaurant but when I got closer I realized it was
    just a café – and not very nice either.
g) I thought it was going to be quite an easy exam, but in actual fact I found
    some of the questions very tricky.
h) I've got a small dictionary which I can use, but I plan to buy a much better
    one when I start my new course.

2 In the sentences below, a person is describing her holiday photos to a friend.
   Complete each sentence with the correct preposition.

a) That's the girl I went ....
b) That's the hotel we stayed ....
c) That's the beach we went ....
d) That's a little village we were shown ....
e) And that's the girl that our guide was planning to get married ....
f) That's a little girl we agreed to look ....
g) That's the island we spent a couple of days ....
h) Oh, and that's the awful waiter we complained ....

Find some holiday photos of your own and try to think of sentences describing the
pictures which end with a preposition (as in the exercise above). Bring them
to school for your next lesson and show them to other members of the class.

3. Write sentences which show the preposition *by* being used with different
    meanings. Compare your answers with a partner in the next lesson.

9 Going places

— 1 —

a The following enquiries and statements were all made at an airport. Read through the list and then answer the questions below.

1 Where do I check in?
2 Which gate is my flight?
3 Which escalator?
4 Can I take these as hand luggage?
5 I've just noticed my passport is out of date. What shall I do?
6 Where have all the trolleys gone?
7 Is there a wheelchair somewhere?
8 Where's the gents?
9 I can't find my boarding card.
10 Do I have to be X-rayed?
11 I can't find a porter.
12 Does it matter if the label comes off?
13 I can't do my zip up.
14 Will the connection wait for me?
15 Is it likely to be a bumpy flight?
16 Do they have nappies on board?
17 Will I have to pay excess baggage?
18 I'm looking for some string.
19 Do they take traveller's cheques in the duty free?
20 What's the star sign of the pilot?

- Which of the enquiries and statements are connected (or probably connected) to a problem with luggage?
- How many of the enquiries might you also hear (a) on a ship and (b) in a hospital?
- How many of the enquiries would you describe as routine, and how many would you describe as unusual?

b Work in groups of eight. Four of you are airport officials and the other four are airline passengers. If you are a passenger, choose four enquiries from above and take them to the different officials. If you are an official, be prepared to answer any of the above enquiries.

— 2 —

a Holiday brochures use a number of adjectives and adverbs to make places sound more attractive. Read the following text and decide where you could insert the words on the right to give a more positive effect.

Champery

Two hours east of Geneva, Champery is situated at the top of the Val d'Illiez, close to the French border. It is a resort set in attractive surroundings on the north side of the valley, and facing the peaks of the Dents-du-Midi. The resort manages to retain all the aspects of a Swiss alpine village, whilst providing excellent winter sports facilities.

ideally
traditional
dramatic
picturesque

Accommodation

Chalet Hermine – is a three-storey chalet. It is built in the style of the traditional Swiss chalet, with its pine walls and open fireplace. Hermine sleeps ten people in one double room and four twin-bedded rooms with two bathrooms and a shower room. It is situated overlooking the village with views of the surrounding countryside.

Chalet sur Cou – is a Swiss farmhouse built in the nineteenth century. It has many features including a cast-iron wood-burning stove and pine furniture, and the owner has retained its charm while modernising it throughout. The chalet sleeps six in one double room and two twin-bedded rooms.

beautiful
luxury
antique
elegant
successfully
breathtaking
original
charming

Skiing in Champery

Champery lies in the heart of the world's largest skiing area, which is aptly named 'Les Portes du Soleil', the gateway to the sun. Les Portes du Soleil has thirteen resorts spread across 400 kilometres of the Swiss-French Alps, with 700 kilometres of marked pistes, all accessible on one ski pass. The region also offers 220 ski lifts, including the 125 person cable car which climbs 1000 metres above Champery to the top of Planachaux. The new cable car has made early morning queues a thing of the past. For beginners the slopes of Planachaux and Les Crosets are starting points, while experts can try the runs such as the World Cup Downhill at Avoriaz/Morzine.

challenging
ideal
gentle
reasonably-priced

b   Find out if any members of your class go skiing. If so, find out where they go, and what it's like. Try and use adjectives from **a**.

—— 3 ——

a Read the following true story. As you read, <u>underline</u> all the words connected with boats and sailing, and(circle)all the verbs which describe one thing hitting another.

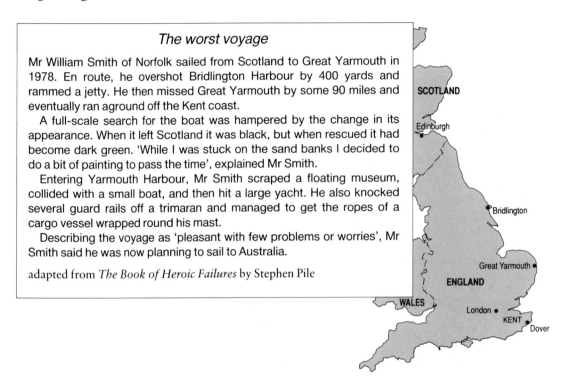

The worst voyage

Mr William Smith of Norfolk sailed from Scotland to Great Yarmouth in 1978. En route, he overshot Bridlington Harbour by 400 yards and rammed a jetty. He then missed Great Yarmouth by some 90 miles and eventually ran aground off the Kent coast.

A full-scale search for the boat was hampered by the change in its appearance. When it left Scotland it was black, but when rescued it had become dark green. 'While I was stuck on the sand banks I decided to do a bit of painting to pass the time', explained Mr Smith.

Entering Yarmouth Harbour, Mr Smith scraped a floating museum, collided with a small boat, and then hit a large yacht. He also knocked several guard rails off a trimaran and managed to get the ropes of a cargo vessel wrapped round his mast.

Describing the voyage as 'pleasant with few problems or worries', Mr Smith said he was now planning to sail to Australia.

adapted from *The Book of Heroic Failures* by Stephen Pile

b Compare your answers with a partner and then complete the following sentences with a suitable word or phrase from the story.

1 I pulled out of the junction without looking and .... with a lorry.
2 The search for the missing girl was .... by the bad weather.
3 The little boy was shivering so I .... a blanket round him.
4 The police have promised a .... investigation into the robbery.
5 I'm sorry I'm late but I got .... in a traffic jam.
6 When I flew to Glasgow we stopped .... to pick up passengers at Manchester.
7 I could just see the ball .... on the surface of the water.
8 It took me ages to .... the dry mud off my boots.

c Making any changes that are necessary, rewrite the above story under the title 'The worst flight' or 'The worst car journey'.

The following words and phrases may help you:

flew   drove   airport   runway   turning   junction
rooftops   ran out of petrol   ran out of fuel   was forced to land
approaching   on the outskirts of   make a crash-landing

SELF-STUDY ACTIVITIES

1a Complete the spaces below with words from the box.

Mount	Lake	Forest	Jungle	Falls
Canal	Desert	Islands	Ocean	Pass

Sahara ....   Panama ....   Atlantic ....   Khyber ....
.... Everest   Niagara ....   Canary ....   Amazon ....
The Black .... Michigan

b Write down one more example of each of the words in the box, and compare your answers with other members of the class in the next lesson.

2 Find a holiday advertisement in a newspaper or travel brochure (in your own language if you are studying in your own country). Underline the key words and phrases which are being used to create a positive impression (and find a translation if it is in your own language), and then compare your answers with other members of the class in the next lesson.

3 Find a word you could use with each of the following pairs.

Example: single or twin-bedded **room**.

a) charter or scheduled ....
b) standby or return ....
c) boarding or landing ....
d) package or sightseeing ....
e) day or business ....
f) tourist or ski ....
g) full or half ....
h) sandy or pebbly ....

10 Affixation

a Form adjectives from the following nouns and complete the table below.

comfort   efficiency   science   fashion   frequency
flexibility   comprehension   accuracy   competence   success
appropriateness   forgiveness   hygiene   faith   help
prediction   convenience   democracy   compatibility

	-able	-ible	-ful	-ent	-ic	-ate
un-	uncomfortable					
in-						

b What general pattern can you see from your answers to **a**? Can you think of any exceptions to this pattern?

c In pairs, decide on an adjective (or adjectives) from **a** to describe the things below. When you have finished compare your answers with another pair.

a watch   a married couple   your best friend
a pair of jeans   a political leader   a meeting at 2.30 p.m.
a cracked cup   a company   an experiment
a society   an old car   a poem
someone's behaviour a bus service   a married man or woman

——— **2** ———

a   Certain prefixes are commonly used with verbs to give a particular meaning. Complete the table below.

Prefix	*Examples*	*Meaning*
un-	unlock, unfold	to reverse an action/process
re-	rewrite, rebuild	
over-		
mis-		

b   Which of the prefixes above can you combine with the following verbs? Use a dictionary to check your answers.

sleep   open   tie   react   elect   examine
behave   screw   charge   design   judge
spend   dress   lead   wrap   pronounce

c   Listen to the five passages on the tape. For each one, write down two things about the passage using the above verbs. Write your answers in the space below. The first one has been started already.

1   The man probably overslept and his boss...
2
3
4
5

——— **3** ———

a   Two or more adjectives are sometimes formed from a noun or verb, and the meanings can become confused. With a partner, discuss the difference in meaning between the following. Use a dictionary to help you.

bored/boring   economic/economical   live/alive/living   classic/classical
childish/childlike   dead/deadly/deathly   alone/lonely   terrific/terrifying
imaginative/imaginary   various/varied

b   **Underline the correct adjective in the following dialogue.**

A: Who do you think is the greatest (live/alive/living) English novelist?

B: Oh, Anthony Burgess, without a doubt.

A: Anthony Burgess? He's (dead/deadly/deathly), isn't he?

B: No I don't think so. At least, he wasn't a couple of weeks ago because I saw him on a(n) (live/alive/living) TV programme, receiving some award.

A: Well, I think his novels are extremely (bored/boring).

B: How can you say that? He's written some (terrific/terrifying) stuff, and his style is so (economic/economical).

A: Yes, but they're all the same.

B: Nonsense. His novels are incredibly (various/varied) and he must certainly be one of the most (imaginative/imaginary) writers this century. There's nothing I like more than being (alone/lonely) on a cold winter's evening with a good Anthony Burgess book.

A: Personally, I'd rather be hit on the head with a (dead/deadly/deathly) weapon than have to read one of his dreary novels.

B: Oh look, you're just being (childish/childlike) now. If you don't appreciate great literature there's no need to be sarcastic. Why don't you run along and play some more pop music on that banjo of yours?

A: It's not a banjo, and I don't play pop music. If you must know, I'm working on a piece by Villa-Lobos – he's a (classic/classical) composer, but I wouldn't expect you to know a thing like that.

SELF-STUDY ACTIVITIES

1   How many words can you find with the prefix *un-* and the suffix *-able*?

Example:
uncomfortable   unsuitable   undrinkable

2   Most of the verbs below form nouns with the addition of *-ion*, but one verb in each group does not. Find the odd man out.

revise	predict	elect	execute	advocate
supervise	conflict	respect	persecute	hesitate
advise	contradict	protect	contribute	illustrate
televise	restrict	reject	commute	demonstrate

3   Prepare a test for your partner using the Word-building tables at the back of the book. Choose ten words from the tables, make sure you know the different parts of the word family in each case, and then test your partner in the next lesson.

Example:
A: What's the noun formed from the verb 'approve'?
B: Approval.

11 Is it right?

a Complete the sentences below with words from the box.

unfair	reasonable	biased	balanced	subjective	fair
prejudiced	neutral	egalitarian	one-sided	objective	

1 That's not .... It's my turn next.
2 She has a totally .... view of the world in which she is always right and everybody else is always wrong.
3 It was quite clear that the referee was .... towards the English team.
4 It was a .... offer and we accepted it.
5 These opinions are all terribly .... Let's look at the facts and try to be .... about it.
6 Some countries remained .... throughout the war.
7 Perhaps everyone is racially .... to some extent.
8 He wrote a very .... report putting both sides of the argument.
9 In a truly .... society there would be no discrimination of any kind.
10 I think it's a little .... of you to blame him for everything that happened.

b With a partner, put the above words into the boxes below, and then compare your answers with another pair.

Positive words
Negative words
Positive or negative

'Tell me again. I've forgotten which way we're supposed to be biased?'

——— 2 ———————————

a Read one of the following texts and complete the grid below for that text. Then, using these notes, explain your text to someone who has read the other text. Use a dictionary to help you.

A

'Humiliated' husband goes free after killing wife during row

A MAN who killed his elderly wife during a row over his burnt dinner received a suspended sentence yesterday.

Mr Frederick Burton, a retired company director, aged 76, was described as a long-suffering husband who was attacked and humiliated by his 79-year-old wife. He believed he had strangled her and tried to commit suicide by taking tablets with whisky.

He regained consciousness the next morning and telephoned the police to tell them what he had done.

Mrs Margaret Burton had died of a heart attack when her husband pressed a nerve in her neck. Only moderate pressure was required, Mold crown court was told, and she died almost immediately.

Mr Burton, of Abergele, north Wales, denied murder. He received a nine-month suspended sentence after admitting manslaughter.

Mr Justice Roch said that Mr Burton had not intended to kill his wife or cause her serious physical harm. "I am satisfied that there had been a momentary loss of control which led you to assault your wife which had tragic and unforeseen consequences," he told Mr Burton.

The judge accepted there had been considerable provocation.

B

Mother who killed to protect daughter escapes jail term

A MOTHER who killed her teenage daughter's boyfriend because he beat the girl up and led her into crime and drug addiction was given a two-year suspended sentence at the Old Bailey yesterday.

Julie Flores, aged 48, was also put on probation after her plea of manslaughter on the grounds of diminished responsibility had been accepted by the court. She had denied murdering Dominic Sparkes, a 28-year-old married man.

The court had heard that Sparkes made her daughter, Renata, pregnant at 15, and that Flores decided to kill him after trying in vain to be rehoused to escape his influence.

Flores hit him over the head last September with a 7lb antique clock weight at her home in Peckham, south London, and then stabbed him 13 times.

Doctors had told the jury how the stress of what had happened to her daughter severely diminished her responsibility.

	Text A	Text B
victim		
accused		
crime		
cause(s) of death		
motive(s)		
sentence		
reason for the light sentence		

b What do you think of the sentence passed by the court in each of these cases? Discuss in groups.

_____ **3** _____

a   Discuss the meaning of the following words and phrases with a partner. Use a dictionary to help you.

to give birth	maternity ward	distraught
to adopt (a child)	identity bracelet	court case
to bring up (a child)	foolproof	legal battle
to be given custody	mix-up	to disrupt
blood test	reveal	to be entitled (to something)

b   The words and phrases in **a** appear in the story below. What do you think the story is about? Discuss your ideas with a partner before you read.

c   Now read the story to see if you were right.

A distraught mother has discovered she has been bringing up the wrong baby for the past six years. And the couple who adopted her real baby are refusing to let her see the boy, saying that he must never be told the truth.

Now heartbroken Jodie is taking the case to court in what is set to be one of America's strangest legal battles over the custody of a child.

The awful truth was revealed when Jodie's marriage began to disintegrate. In one of their many rows, husband Walter claimed he was not the real father of their son. Blood tests not only proved him right, but also showed that Jodie could not be the real mother.

Further investigations revealed a tragic mix-up at Griffith Hospital where Jodie had given birth. The hospital's supposedly foolproof system of identity bracelets had gone wrong, and somewhere between the maternity ward and the nursery two babies were switched. Jodie's real child was given to a young mother who had already arranged for her baby to be adopted. And the couple who adopted the boy, and named him Melvin, are now saying that the young boy's life would be too badly disrupted if he ever saw Jodie and learned the truth.

Meanwhile Jodie has now officially adopted the child she has been looking after for six years. But yesterday she vowed: 'I'll fight to the end to get Melvin back. I'm entitled to have him – he's my son.'

d   Divide into groups of four, two of you representing Jodie, and two of you representing Melvin's adoptive parents. Each side must present the arguments in support of the people they represent.

SELF-STUDY ACTIVITIES
---

1 The following sentences are not right. Can you find the mistake in each one and correct it?

   a) It is not allowed to smoke in theatres in England.
   b) My knowledge in the legal system is very poor.
   c) I went to England to do a stage in Constitutional Law.
   d) She denied to start the fire.
   e) In the most countries it is illegal to drive without insurance.
   f) The officials will control your passport at the border.
   g) When parents separate I feel sorry about the children.
   h) She tried to suicide.
   i) According to my opinion rapists should go to prison for at least ten years.
   j) You can be persecuted if you trespass on someone's property.

2 Find a story (from a newspaper or from your own experience) which demonstrates bias, prejudice or unfairness. Be prepared to tell the story in your next lesson.

3 Complete the sentences below with words from the box.

recognize	deny	surrender	get away	conform
condemn	ignore	retaliate	tighten up	release

   a) He admitted killing the man but .... it was murder.
   b) They may rebel at first but they will soon learn to ....
   c) I wouldn't condone their action but neither would I .... it entirely.
   d) Some soldiers are continuing to fight but the majority have ....
   e) He provoked me and I ....
   f) I tried to warn her but she just .... me.
   g) One of the policemen chased after them but they ....
   h) Two men were detained but the others were ....
   i) He tried to disguise himself but he was soon ....
   j) The rules have been relaxed far too much, so we will certainly .... the legislation.

12 Revision and expansion

─── **1** ───────────────

Complete the spaces in the sentences below with suitable words.
Example:

pilots fly _planes_.

1 .... spend hours marking ....
2 .... commit ....
3 .... buy and sell ....
4 .... bring up ....
5 .... sentence ....
6 .... elect ....
7 .... lend ....
8 .... obey ....
9 .... recruit ....
10 .... cancel ....

─── **2** ───────────────

Put the following words on the map below. You may put words inside a
circle, between circles, or wherever you like. When you have finished,
compare your answers with a partner and discuss the differences.

save   examine   victim   undress   stressful   prejudiced
unlock   hostile   helpful   under scrutiny   successful
disrupt   hygienic   inflexible   encouragement   pregnant

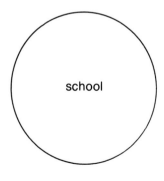

school

prison

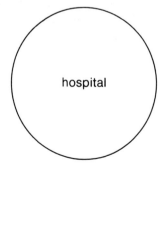

hospital

———— **3** ————

Which is the odd man out in each of the following groups of words? Work with a partner and be prepared to explain your answers to another pair.

1 attack someone   assault someone   threaten someone   beat someone up
2 stab someone   poison someone   shoot someone   strangle someone
3 demanding   challenging   tiring   rewarding
4 luxury   antique   original   traditional
5 be promoted   resign   be sacked   retire
6 salesman   politician   vet   vicar

———— **4** ————

Complete the following sentences with a suitable verb or adjective.

1 We're .... of going to Greece next year.
2 I know it sounds silly but I've always been .... of the dark.
3 He's not very .... in art so I shouldn't think we'll go to the gallery.
4 I'm really .... to seeing their new house.
5 I was really .... by the scenes of violence in the film.
6 He's never been very .... at maths; he failed all his exams at school.
7 I couldn't eat the starter because I'm .... to seafood.
8 Some children can be extremely irritating but I've always been very .... of Joanne.
9 I'm getting very .... about my driving test; I'm sure I'm going to fail.
10 I wish I could offer you a drink but I'm afraid I've just .... of tea and coffee.

———— **5** ————

a **Divide the following words into two groups: words with the stress on the first syllable and words with the stress on the second syllable.**

◯ ₒ	ₒ ◯

voyage   channel   canal
dessert   desert   commute
average   cottage   antique
resort   hotel   hazard
addict   collide   recruit

b 📼 **Listen and check your answers.**

—— **6** ——

Complete the following network and then extend it in any way you like.
Show the result to a partner.

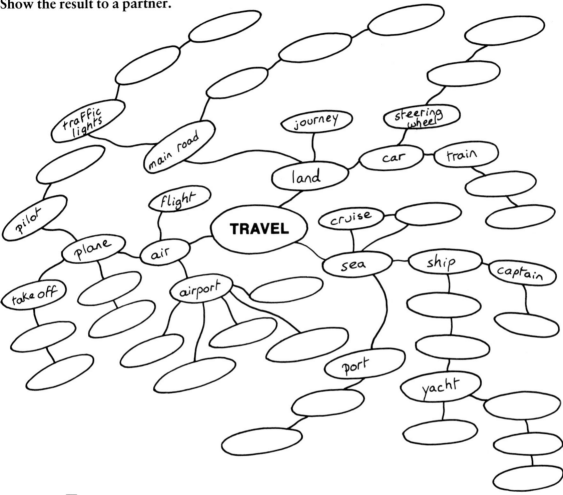

—— **7** ——

Here is a quiz to test your memory on Units 7–11. Work with a partner, and
then exchange your answers with another pair.

1 In Unit 7 you read about some of the causes and effects of stress. How many
   can you remember?
2 In Unit 9 a man had an unhappy experience sailing down the east coast of
   England. What happened?
3 In Unit 10 two people had an argument about Anthony Burgess. What was
   the argument about, and what did each person think?
4 In Unit 11 you read about two cases of manslaughter. Can you remember the
   details?
5 Also in Unit 11 you read about the tragic story of Jodie and her son. What
   happened?

―― **8** ――――――――――――――――――――――――

a With a partner, prepare a story using all of the things shown below.

b Tell another student your story.

―― **9** ――――――――――――――――――――――――

How many words can you find beginning with one of the prefixes on the left,
and ending with one of the suffixes on the right?

Prefixes	Suffixes	
in-	-ate	-ent
un-	-able	-ic(al)

—— 10 ——

Work in groups of four. Choose one preposition each from the list on the left, and then take it in turns to make up sentences using your preposition and a word from the list on the right. You cannot use a word from the right-hand list more than once, and if you make up a sentence which is incorrect, you must drop out of the game.

	holiday	accuse	first	way	all	take
at	sudden	earth	apologize	look	random
on	glance	time	congratulate	blame	least
of	thank	strike	remind	run out	lack
for	good	sudden	mistake	end	outskirts
	date	last				

—— 11 ——

With a partner, write down eighteen jobs which begin with different letters of the alphabet. When you have finished, compare your answers with the list of jobs and professions on page 29.

—— 12 ——

This activity will help you with 'problem' words. Spend a few minutes looking through your notes and the previous five units, and then complete the columns below with some examples.

I can't pronounce:	I'm not sure of the meaning of:	I'm not sure how to use:	I find . . . difficult to remember.

Move round the class to see if other students can help you with your words and give you useful suggestions about pronouncing, learning, using and remembering them.

13 Newspapers

—— 1 ———————————————————

a The following text gives information and opinions about English newspapers. Read the first part and then answer the question below.

England has eleven national daily newspapers. Of these, five represent the 'quality' press: papers aimed largely at the middle-class audience, and providing detailed coverage of politics, finance and the arts. The remaining six represent the 'popular' press and are all tabloids, i.e. small in size. These papers tend to concentrate more on human interest stories, although they are sometimes criticized for prying into the private lives of famous people – notably the Royal Family.

Would you expect to find the following in a quality paper, a popular paper, or both?

theatre reviews   gossip column   cartoons   overseas news
adverts for BMW cars   adverts for self-assembly kitchen units
weather forecast   stock market prices   pin-ups

b Now read the second part of the text and do the exercise after it.

It is often said that the press in England has become more right-wing in recent years. Only two papers would now claim to be left of centre, while a majority express views which are, to a large extent, consistent with the philosophy of the Conservative party in Great Britain. In view of the power of the press to influence public opinion, this bias is regarded by some people as unhealthy and potentially dangerous. Others might argue that newspapers do not dictate public opinion, they simply reflect it and express the views of the majority.

The text uses a number of words and phrases to modify an opinion which other people may not agree with, e.g. the writer says 'the quality press: aimed *largely* at a middle-class audience'. Find other words and phrases in the text which perform the same function and then use them to modify the following statements:

1 Television glamorizes violence.
2 She's a communist.
3 All newspapers are biased.
4 It's a democratic country.
5 People believe what they read in the newspapers.
6 Expensive clothes are just a status symbol.

c In groups, discuss newspapers in your own country. Are they largely national or regional? Do they tend to be right-wing or left-wing? Is there the same distinction between a quality press and a popular press?

2

a The opening sentences of a newspaper story often paraphrase words used in the headline and expand the information. Match the following headlines with the stories below, and underline the words and phrases in the stories which paraphrase or expand the headlines.

1 **Amnesty alleges mass state killings**

2 Seven hurt in blast at warehouse

3 US calls for big curb on farm subsidies

4 Lawyers and doctors urged to double as clergymen

5 **NUS leader quits over hard left**

6 Channel 4 drops live TV plan

7 **Improved lighting cuts crime by 90%**

8 Sudan junta chief pledge

a)

Amnesty International says government agents were responsible for the deliberate killing of tens of thousands of people in at least two dozen countries in 1988, and such killings have continued this year.

b)

THE US government yesterday proposed sweeping reductions in agricultural subsidies and trade barriers worldwide, including the abolition of all farm export subsidies over five years.

c)

DOCTORS, lawyers and mechanics are among professionals being encouraged to become part-time ministers to overcome a shortage of Church of England clergy.

d)

CHANNEL 4 has decided against regular live broadcasts from the Commons for the time being, because it believes viewers would get poor coverage under restrictions imposed by MPs. But the channel is launching a second regular parliamentary programme.

e) A SENIOR member of the National Union of Students has resigned because he says the hard left has taken over.

f)

Households in an inner London neighbourhood experienced a drop of more than 90 per cent in crimes like burglary and vandalism after street lighting was improved, according to research published today.

g)

GENERAL Omar Hassan al-Bashir, the leader of Sudan's junta, has promised to launch a military offensive against rebels in the south of the country following his first major setback since seizing power in a coup in June.

h) Seven people were hurt, one of them seriously, in an explosion at a warehouse in Brentwood, Essex, last night.

⟫→

b Create six possible headlines using the words in the list below.
Example:

> *Commuters urge new rail link or Government drops new rail link*

commuters	newspaper	pledge(s)	air fares	support	US
drop(s)	at	government	launch	blast	in	peace plan
allege(s)	minister	hotel	Pan-Am	for	BMW	curb(s)
corruption	China	quit(s)	doctors	bomb	by	new model
cut(s)	new drug	new rail link	urge		

c Write the first sentence of the stories for each headline, and then see if a partner can guess your headlines.

—— **3** ——————————————————————————

a Complete the texts below using a suitable word or phrase in each space. All of the missing words are repeated somewhere in the texts, so you should be able to find the answers.

Ambulance staff step up pay action

AMBULANCE crews throughout the country .... their work-to-rule action from midnight last night in support of their six-week pay dispute.

There will be tighter restrictions on the movement of staff from station to station, on shift arrangements and on replacements when staff are on holiday.

Union ...., who meet tomorrow to discuss further action, have said they will continue to provide accident and .... services.

The Army was put on standby when .... between the health employers and the unions at Acas, the conciliation service, broke down last week. But a spokesman for Nupe, the union leading the ...., warned that ambulance staff could stage sit-ins at stations if .... were called in.

from The Independent

Ambulance chaos set to worsen

THE six-week-old ambulance dispute looks set to .... this week, with the Government preparing to use troops to maintain services.

.... leaders, who meet tomorrow to discuss further action, have pledged they will keep accident and emergency services going.

But strict work-to-rule .... could be introduced.

The Army was put on .... last week when pay talks between the health employers and the unions at Acas, the conciliation service, ...

Police were .... to answer emergency calls during a short-lived overtime ban by London ambulancemen.

b Using all the missing words from **a**, write your own short newspaper text based on the following problem.

Air traffic controllers have now been on a work-to-rule for three weeks. They asked for a nine per cent rise but have been offered five per cent. They are meeting employers next week and have threatened to call an all-out strike if the offer is not increased.

SELF-STUDY ACTIVITIES

1 If you are studying English in your own country, you will probably see the news on television at least one day before English papers for that day arrive in your country. So, watch the news, choose a story that interests you, and then write down key words and phrases from the news report (you can do the same thing from a newspaper in your own language the following morning). Try to find English equivalents for these words and phrases and then buy an English paper which reports the same news story. Look for your English equivalents or any other words and phrases which seem important to the story.

   This activity will help you to build up vocabulary around topics that interest you.

2 Here are some more words commonly used in newspaper headlines. Find a synonym (or paraphrase) for each of the underlined words.

   Example:

   ## PM to hold <u>key</u> talks   key = important

   Bush <u>backs</u> crackdown on drugs   New famine <u>threat</u>

   Two Britons <u>held</u>   Cabinet <u>split</u> on wealth tax

   New food <u>scare</u>   Trade <u>gap</u> widens

3 Newspapers sometimes make amusing typographical errors. Can you find the mistakes in the following?

   a) Goalkeeper, Stepney, saved an almost certain goal when he died at the feet of Davies.
   b) GOOD HOME WANTED for beautiful black and white male kitchen.
   c) Greg Norman missed a five-inch putt at the 11th green yesterday. The blind Australian tried to tap in the ball one-handed but hit the ground instead.
   d) There was white bread only and apart from the soap everything was overcooked.
   e) Borchardt is accused of disturbing the peace by hurling a choir against the window of the Turkish cultural centre.
   f) It was in the same stadium last year that Ade Mafe first hit the headlines by eating the American sprinter Mel Lattany in the 200 metres.

14 Verbs

1
---

a One verb in each list below is an odd man out, and for a similar reason.
Which verb is it, and what is the reason?

bleed	let	bend	blink	know
feed	get	send	stink	throw
need	bet	lend	drink	show
breed	upset	mend	sink	blow

b Which verb (or verbs) from **a** are you likely to find in a sentence with the
following nouns? Write a sentence for each noun containing one of the above
verbs and read your sentences to a partner.

horses   baby   ship   £5   race   wind   knee   socks

2
---

a In each of the questions below, three of the answers are correct and one
is wrong. Underline the wrong answer.

1 He .... us to go to a Chinese restaurant.
   a) advised   b) suggested   c) wanted   d) told
2 She .... me to take the exam.
   a) encouraged   b) persuaded   c) insisted   d) begged
3 He .... us to leave.
   a) told   b) allowed   c) forced   d) made
4 I don't .... seeing them.
   a) mind   b) expect   c) remember   d) regret
5 I .... working with him.
   a) agreed   b) enjoyed   c) avoided   d) loathed
6 She .... me move the furniture.
   a) made   b) let   c) helped   d) wanted
7 I .... to start work after the holidays.
   a) hope   b) am thinking   c) agreed   d) expect
8 They .... that I should stay at their house.
   a) suggested   b) wanted   c) proposed   d) insisted
9 He .... that it was very dangerous.
   a) told   b) pointed out   c) mentioned   d) said
10 I'm .... working with him.
   a) thinking of   b) used to   c) hoping to   d) looking forward to

b   What changes are necessary to make grammatically correct sentences using the underlined verbs?

c   The above sentences show seven constructions that can be used with particular verbs. What are those seven constructions?

—— **3** ——

a   Find the seven pairs of words and phrases in this list which are similar in meaning.

look for   reach a climax   stab someone   arrive   give oneself up
let me go   try to find   turn up   release me   come to a head
attack someone with a knife   leave me alone   surrender   go away

b   Below is the story of *Carmen*, an opera by Bizet. As you read it notice how some of the words and phrases from **a** are used. Look up any other new words in a dictionary.

CARMEN
INFLUENCE

Carmen is a gypsy temptress who works in a cigar factory. Into town wanders another woman called Micheala, looking for her man Don José, an army corporal. When Carmen stabs another woman in a fight outside the factory Don José arrests her, but she persuades him to let her go. He goes to jail himself for his leniency. Later Carmen is visiting a tavern with her smuggler friends when Don José turns up there and she seduces him. Another of Carmen's suitors, Escamillo, the toreador, arrives and fights with Don José over Carmen. When Escamillo leaves, Carmen tries to follow him but Don José bars her way. The passionate triangle comes to a head at the bullfight. As Escamillo enters in triumph Don José intercepts Carmen as she goes to watch. Carmen tells him to leave her alone or kill her. Famous last words . . . he stabs her to death, then gives himself up.

》》》→

c 🔲 Now listen to the man telling the story of *Carmen*. His account is different from the above text in three ways. What are they?

d With a partner, write your own version of *Carmen* but set the story in your own country in the 1990s. What changes will be necessary or desirable?

—— **4** ——————————————————————

a Many verbs have a literal meaning and a more abstract or figurative meaning.

Example:
   We had to <u>bend</u> the pipe in order to remove it.
   We had to <u>bend</u> the rules to give her a place. (= to break the rules slightly)

Complete the sentences a–h using the underlined verbs in the sentences 1–8.

1 The horse managed to <u>jump</u> the fence.
2 We had to get down on hands and knees and <u>crawl</u> along the tunnel.
3 The money <u>slipped through</u> a hole in my pocket.
4 The lights <u>flashed</u> on and off but I couldn't see him clearly.
5 Our feet were tied together so we couldn't <u>go far</u>.
6 The fire <u>spread</u> quickly to the second floor.
7 The man <u>grabbed</u> my handbag and ran off.
8 The door's <u>stuck</u> so we may have to get out through the window.

a) The rumour soon .... throughout the school.
b) An idea suddenly .... across my mind.
c) Several people tried to .... the queue, which was very annoying.
d) The terrorists somehow managed to .... the security checks.
e) It was the rush hour so we just .... along the main road out of town.
f) I've done most of the exercise but I'm .... on the last question.
g) I'm afraid £5 doesn't .... these days.
h) You must .... your chance now, otherwise it may be too late.

b Which of the above verbs would be likely to appear in each of the following newspaper stories? Work with a partner.

Collapsed bridge causes traffic chaos
Fears grow of new flu epidemic
Crew rescued from burning tanker
Passengers describe hostage drama
Opposition MPs attack immigration policy
Bank robbers escape with £2m

SELF-STUDY ACTIVITIES

1 Find ten irregular verbs which you think are difficult to remember. In your next lesson, test a partner on the past tense and past participle of these verbs, and be prepared to explain the meaning if necessary.

2 Some verbs can be followed by two objects, for example:

| He gave | me | the money. |
| She reserved | him | a ticket. |

Complete the following sentences with a suitable object.

a) She lent me ....
b) He poured me ....
c) I owe him ....
d) She saved me ....

e) She cashed me ....
f) He booked me ....
g) They offered me ....
h) He threw me ....

3 Choose the best synonym from the following for the meaning of *see* in the sentences below.

make sure   picture   understand
witness   find out   accompany

a) I don't know what it means but I'll see what it says in the dictionary.
b) I said I would see her home as it was quite late.
c) I would like to see a number of changes in the company.
d) I can't really see myself as a soldier.
e) Don't worry, I'll see that they get home safely.
f) I see what you mean, but I'm not sure I entirely agree.

Look up the verb *see* in a good monolingual dictionary and try to find these six different meanings. How would you translate these different meanings of *see* into your own language?

How we see flowers

How they see themselves

15 Choices

1

a There are many common phrases used to express *choice* and *preference*.
Examples:

I'd (much) prefer <u>Hungary</u> to <u>Poland.</u>
I'd (much) prefer to <u>go to Hungary.</u>
I'd (much) rather <u>go to Hungary.</u>

If I had | the choice, / to choose, | I'd | pick / go for <u>the blue one.</u>

I don't think there's much to choose between <u>the brown one and the yellow one.</u>

I don't like / I wouldn't want | either / any | of them.

b In groups, decide which you would choose or prefer from the following:

1 A noisy hotel room overlooking the beach *or* a quiet room overlooking a back street with a row of shops?
2 A £500 computer *or* a £500 hi-fi?
3 A two-week cruise in the Caribbean *or* a two-week holiday on a safari park in Kenya?
4 A filling at the dentist's *or* an injection at the doctor's?
5 A dishwasher *or* a microwave?
6 A car with a sunroof *or* a car with central locking and electric windows?
7 A monolingual dictionary *or* a bilingual dictionary?
8 To drive in a storm *or* to drive in fog?
9 To get wet *or* to get cold?
10 To live near the centre of town *or* to live on the outskirts of town?

Vending machines of the Serengeti

—— **2** ————————————————————————————

a Complete the sentences below with a suitable word. To help you, all of the answers are contained (vertically or horizontally) in the word puzzle on the right.

1 In the lounge we're not sure whether to have a fitted carpet or just varnish the floor and put down some ....

2 And we can't make up our minds whether to have curtains or ....

3 We haven't decided yet whether to paint the walls or put up ....

4 In the alcove beside the fireplace we might build a cupboard or we could build some ....

5 On the bathroom floor we don't know whether to have a carpet or ....

L	A	W	N	T	I	L	E	S
O	B	A	S	E	M	E	N	T
B	A	L	C	O	N	Y	C	E
L	S	L	C	E	L	L	A	R
I	O	P	A	T	I	O	F	R
N	F	A	R	U	G	S	E	A
D	A	P	L	O	F	T	N	C
S	H	E	L	V	E	S	C	E
W	A	R	D	R	O	B	E	D

6 In the main bedroom we were thinking of having a built-in .... Alternatively we could just buy one.

7 As we often have guests we'll either get a double bed for the spare room or buy a ....-bed to save space.

8 At the back of the house we were thinking of building a conservatory. Alternatively we could just put down a stone floor and use it as a ....

9 In the centre of the garden we can't make up our minds whether to have flower beds or a ....

10 Around the garden we might dig up the hedge and put up a ....

b If it were your house, what would you choose to do in each case? Discuss in groups.

c In the word puzzle above, can you find at least five more words which describe parts or features of a house?

———— **3** ————

a   You are going to listen to a man talking about the different ways he can get to work. Before you listen, write down phrases in which the following verbs are likely to appear.

catch   take   get   run   work out

b   [cassette icon]   Now listen and see if your phrases are used. Write down additional phrases containing these verbs and try to decide what they mean.

c   Complete the chart below. If necessary, listen to the tape again.

	Advantages	Disadvantages
by bus		
by tube		
by car		
by bike		

d   If it were you, which form of transport would you choose? Discuss in groups.

e   Tell a partner the different ways you can get to work or school. Try and use as many expressions from the tape as possible.

SELF-STUDY ACTIVITIES
---

1 Choose adjectives from the left which combine with nouns on the right to
form common word combinations. (Adjectives may combine with more than
one noun.)

furnished	high	damp	iron	cellar	garden	gate	house
sheltered	patterned	velvet		curtains	kitchen	floor	
terraced	fitted	concrete		wallpaper	flat	ceiling	

2 If you were buying a car, what factors would influence you the most? Rank the
factors below as very important, quite important or not important.

performance (i.e. speed and acceleration)   colour
reputation for safety   looks
reputation for reliability   price
equipment (e.g. sunroof, central locking)   comfort
reputation for construction   image
low depreciation   other?

3 Choose one of the following techniques for vocabulary learning and use it
over the next week. In a week's time you can discuss the results in class and
discover what each person has learned.

a) Look through your notes and find five words that you had forgotten. Write
these words down on a piece of paper and put it in your pocket. Look at
your list for one minute every day to try and remember the words.
Tomorrow you can do the same thing for five more words, but put the
words on a different piece of paper and in a different pocket.

b) At the end of each day write down what you have eaten that day. Use a
bilingual dictionary to help you. You could do the same thing for the
weather each day, conversations you have with people, what you spend
money on, etc.

c) If you travel to work or school by train or bus, describe what you can see
on the journey in English. Make a note of anything you can't say in English,
and find out the English before your next day's journey. Keep a record of
all the new words and expressions you learn.

16 Connecting words and ideas

──── 1 ────

a Complete the text below with a suitable word or phrase from the following:

however   in view of   provided (that)   in spite of   moreover
in view of the fact that   although   unless   of course

Chairman's Report

I am pleased to announce that we have had a very successful year .... difficult market conditions. Overall, profits have reached £80 million, which is particularly pleasing .... interest rates have remained high throughout the year. .... we have not suffered the decline in sales which has so badly affected some other sectors of the retail market.

The one disappointment has been in Scotland where we have made a loss of almost £4 million. ...., we are now making considerable improvements to the services we will be able to offer our customers in Glasgow and Edinburgh, and .... we are able to complete our rebuilding programme by mid-April, I am optimistic that we will reverse these disappointing results by the time of my next annual report.

............, our success would not have been possible without the dedication of the staff throughout the country; and I would like to take this opportunity to thank everyone for their continued loyalty and support.

b Now replace three of your answers with the words and phrases you have not used. Make any changes to the text that are necessary.

c With a partner, write your own examples using these link words and phrases, and include the word *examination* in each one. When you have finished move round the class and compare your examples.

—— **2** ———————————————————————

a   Replace the underlined phrases in the sentences below with a suitable adverb from the following:

recently   luckily   eventually   hopefully   apparently
presumably   originally   potentially   ideally   generally

Example:
   A: Have you been to the museum?
   B: No, not <u>in the last few months.</u> *recently*

1 A: You can't buy the tickets until the day of the concert, then?
   B: <u>I'm not absolutely sure, but that's what I've heard.</u>
2 A: Do you always carry your cheque book around with you?
   B: Yes, <u>most of the time.</u>
3 A: You want a flat in central London with a garden.
   B: Yes, <u>that would be perfect.</u>
4 A: John arrived, then?
   B: Yes, <u>after I'd waited for over an hour.</u>
5 A: You found your wallet, then?
   B: Yes, <u>I was lucky.</u>
6 A: Do you think you'll find your wallet?
   B: Yes, <u>with a bit of luck.</u>
7 A: You live in Italy, but you actually come from Spain, don't you?
   B: Yes, <u>that's where I was born and brought up.</u>
8 A: Did he buy the suit specially for the wedding?
   B: Well, I suppose so. <u>I can't think of any other reason for him to buy it.</u>
9 A: You think he's a good player, then?
   B: Well, <u>he has the ability to be a good player in the future.</u>

b   These adverbs are also used to link ideas in a sentence (and between sentences) to give additional information or to express our attitude.
Complete the following sentences using the adverbs in **a**.

Example:
   I used to visit my uncle a lot, but . . . *recently I haven't seen him very much*

1 I left my keys in the car, but . . .
2 The food wasn't very good last night, but . . .
3 The job doesn't pay much at the moment, but . . .
4 I may be forced to buy a second-hand car, but . . .
5 I thought it was free, but . . .
6 It's a popular tourist resort now, but . . .
7 We may have to modify the scheme a bit, but . . .
8 It's not an easy exam, but . . .
9 She didn't actually say when she'd be back, but . . .

c   Compare your answers with a partner and discuss any differences.

3

a **Look at the way vocabulary is being used to connect the conversation in the following examples:**

A: Will you get <u>lunch</u> and <u>dinner</u>?
B: Yes, they provide all <u>meals</u>.

A: Can I get by with a <u>hammer</u> and <u>screwdriver</u>?
B: No, you'll need a complete set of <u>tools</u>.

Write a suitable response to the following sentences using a more general word in your answer. If you don't know the correct word, you will find the answers in the box on p. 70.

1 Can you get it in cotton and silk?
2 If you're not a member, are you still allowed to use the bar and the sauna?
3 Did the company pay for your hotel and travel?
4 Was the wheat damaged as badly as the fruit?
5 The project will require a lot of land, a huge labour force, and considerable energy and patience.
6 They keep dogs, cats and rabbits, don't they?
7 Do you want us to put the ropes, torches and hammer in the tent?
8 Do you get a lot of ants and cockroaches in the summer?
9 Were they carrying guns and knives?
10 Do they want you to move all of your furniture out of the flat, as well as your clothes and stuff?

b **Practise similar dialogues in reverse. Ask your partner a question using one of the general words, and see if they can give you a suitable answer using more specific vocabulary.**

Example:
   A: Did you have all your tools in the car?
   B: No, just a couple of screwdrivers.

Let's see – Mosquitoes, gnats, flies, ants . . . What the? . . . Those jerks! We didn't order stink bugs on this thing!'

—— 4 ——

a   Some English words have a very general meaning in isolation, but in context they become more specific and serve to represent ideas in a text and connect them.

Example:

A: He is very bad at <u>organizing his time</u> and doesn't seem to realize the importance of this <u>aspect</u> of the job. I'd love to get rid of him.

B: I thought <u>he was the chairman's nephew.</u>

A: Yes he is. Under these <u>circumstances</u> I may simply have to <u>have a quiet word with him.</u>

B: Mmm. I'm not sure that <u>approach</u> will do much good.

A: No, neither am I.

b   What is the general meaning of the underlined words in the following text, and what are the specific ideas they refer to?

In a new attempt to ease traffic congestion in London, the Transport Secretary has proposed a series of underground roads linking major routes into the capital, plus a programme of road improvements which would widen existing roads.

These <u>measures</u> are certain to meet with considerable hostility from residents in the affected areas, and so the government is planning a number of open meetings to try and win public support for the <u>scheme</u> before going ahead with it. Few believe this <u>approach</u> will satisfy opponents to the <u>proposal</u>, but the government has stated its firm intention to tackle an <u>issue</u> which is now becoming critical. It is estimated that the number of cars on our roads could double within 25 years: at this <u>rate</u>, traffic in major cities could soon be brought to a complete standstill.

An increase in roadbuilding will also anger environmental groups, who support large-scale investment in public transport to reduce pollution levels and minimize the destruction of the Green Belt around London. 'Unfortunately', said a spokesman for *Friends of the Earth*, 'these <u>aspects</u> of urban planning are quickly swept aside when there is a danger of antagonizing private motorists.'

The Transport Secretary, however, will not want to be seen as unsympathetic to the demands of environmental groups, so he is faced with a <u>dilemma</u> which is certain to ensure a bumpy road ahead – whatever the outcome.

SELF-STUDY ACTIVITIES

1 Answer the following questions and compare your answers in class in the next lesson.

What are the main crops grown in your country?
What are the most common insects found in your country?
What are the most important natural resources in your country?
What are the most famous export goods produced in your country?
What are the technical facilities that your school provides?

2 The words and phrases below could be used in place of the six answers to exercise **1a** in this unit. Put them into the correct place in the text.

considering (that)   as long as   needless to say
in addition   but   despite

3 While you are reading newspapers or novels in your own language, make a note of five important link words or phrases which you can't express in English. Use a dictionary to try and find the English equivalents, and discuss your findings with other members of the class and your teacher in a future lesson.

Here are the words you need for Exercise 3a.

1 material	2 facilities	3 expenses	4 crops	5 resources
6 pets	7 equipment	8 insects	9 weapons	10 belongings

17   Technology

— 1

a Which words from the box are being defined in the sentences below?

television	microphone	speedometer	physiotherapy
telephone	microchip	barometer	psychotherapy
telex	microscope	thermometer	radio
telescope	microbiology	thermostat	radiology
	microwave	thermodynamics	

1 A system for sending written messages to another by telephone line.
2 An instrument for measuring air pressure.
3 A device that automatically controls a heating system.
4 An instrument which magnifies very small objects.
5 A branch of medical science involving the use of radioactivity in examining and treating disease.
6 The treatment of people using movement and exercise.

b Complete the following definitions of words from the box, using vocabulary from the sentences in **a**.

1 A(n) .... for .... temperature.
2 A(n) .... that you speak into to record or amplify your voice.
3 The .... of illness .... psychology rather than drugs.
4 A(n) .... for .... or receiving sound, especially speech, over long distances by electrical means.
5 A(n) .... which makes distant objects appear larger and nearer.
6 A(n) .... of .... which .... the relationship between heat and other forms of energy.

c Now complete your own definitions for the words below. Work with a partner, then compare your answers with another pair and the dictionary definitions.

a microwave   a speedometer   a radio

2

a In groups, try and decide the functions of the gadgets in the pictures below. What are they? How do they work? What are their special features?

1

2

3

4

5

6

7

8

b Compare your answers with another group and write down their answers. If you are unable to express an idea in English, write down a translation or a paraphrase in English.

c One group can now read a description of four of the gadgets below, while the other group reads the description of the other four gadgets on p. 124. As you read, pay special attention to new vocabulary, particularly words and phrases needed to explain the functions of the gadgets.

Under pressure?

Driving on the wrong pressure could cost you far more than the cost of new tyres – because it's also highly dangerous. And garage forecourt gauges are notoriously inaccurate. Now, thanks to this ingenious new hi-tech device, you can minimise the risks. What makes this Sonic Accutyre so different is that you simply slip it over the valve, press a button and a beep tells you when the pressure has been recorded. Then simply read the measurement on the clear LCD display. Easy to use and very accurate, this neat piece of technology runs on just one lithium battery which should last for 10 years.

The first cordless travel iron

This is the best travel iron we've seen, because it can be used anywhere with no need for an electric power source or batteries. The secret is in the special water activated heating sachets – just insert one into the iron, add water and the iron will start to heat up. One sachet will give you about 20 minutes' ironing time, at a heat suitable for most lightweight fabrics. The iron has a stainless steel base and comes with full instructions. For travelling the handle folds neatly away.

The staple-less stapler

Paperlok is a new way of attaching papers together using no staples at all. It punches two distinctive holes through the paper which fix and tab them together. It attaches them just as strongly as a conventional stapler and will take up to 5 sheets at a time. When you want to remove the tabs they tear off neatly.

Remove unwanted hair hygienically

If you care about good grooming it's essential to remove unwanted hair from the nose, ears and eyebrows. This new battery operated Clipper will complete the task for you quickly and painlessly. Its slim style ensures that it is convenient and easy to use and its head can be removed for cleaning by brushing or blowing. It operates on one AA battery (not supplied).

3

a Make sure you understand the words in the list below. Use a dictionary if necessary.

television   photocopier   food mixer   washing machine
vacuum cleaner   computer   radio   electric drill
printer   camera   dishwasher   typewriter   speakers

b 🔲 Listen to the conversations and decide which object is being talked about in each case. Use the right-hand column in the table below for key words and phrases which helped you decide upon your answer.

Object	*How do you know?*
1	
2	
3	
4	
5	
6	

c 🔲 Listen to the tape again and write down any further words and phrases which might be used to describe a problem with a machine or appliance. Discuss your answers with a partner.

Example:

> The first conversation talks about 'interference'. This could be true of a radio as well as a television, but nothing else in the box.

d Answer the following questions and then discuss your answers in groups.

1 The picture keeps flickering on your TV. Would you:
   a) turn it off?
   b) fiddle with the knobs to try and fix it yourself?
   c) get someone else to have a look at it?

2 You get a puncture on a quiet country road. Would you:
   a) change the wheel yourself?
   b) go and look for a telephone?
   c) try and wave down a passing motorist?

3 Somebody showed you how the photocopier works but you still don't fully understand. Would you:
   a) try and work it out for yourself?
   b) ask the person to show you again?
   c) ask a different person to explain it to you?

4 You've just bought a video but you're not sure how to tune it in. Would you:
   a) try and work it out for yourself?
   b) follow the instruction manual carefully?
   c) ask someone to do it for you?

5 A radiator in your hotel room is leaking a little bit. Would you:
   a) try and fix it yourself?
   b) report it to reception?
   c) do nothing unless it was inconveniencing you?

4

a 🔊 Read through the descriptions of different sounds below and then listen to the examples for each one. They are in the same order as the list.

1 a buzzing noise
2 a kind of screeching sound
3 a ticking sound
4 a creaking sound
5 a drilling noise
6 a hammering sound
7 a banging noise
8 a hissing sound

b Try and reproduce these noises yourself and see if a partner can guess which one you are making.

c With the same partner, write down things that often make these noises (but not in the same order). Give your list to a different pair and see if they can match the noises with the items on your list.

SELF-STUDY ACTIVITIES

1 What word(s) could be used after each of the following pairs of adjectives?

Example: cordless or steam .*iron*....

a) brand new or second-hand ....
b) auto-focus or zoom ....
c) hard or floppy ....
d) laser or dot matrix ....

e) digital or analogue ....
f) record or tape ....
g) mains or portable ....
h) manual or automatic ....

2 Find an interesting gadget at home, and make sure you can explain what it is and how it works. Bring it to class in your next lesson and see if other members of the class can identify it and explain its function.

3 One of the best ways to record the meaning of words which describe sounds is to make a cassette recording yourself. Try recording the following sounds onto cassette:

a) someone whistling
b) someone humming
c) a dog barking

d) someone screaming
e) someone mumbling
f) a dog howling

g) someone whispering
h) someone tapping
i) a dog growling

In a few day's time, listen to the sounds and write down what you can hear. This is a good way to test yourself on vocabulary and you can also bring your cassette to class and test other members of the class.

18 Revision and expansion

1

Writers often repeat ideas in a text, but they usually avoid repeating the same words and phrases. Complete the following sentences using a synonym for the word or phrase in italics.

1 They *send* us the information and we .... it to the central computer.
2 It *eases* pain and .... stress.
3 You should have *gone the quick way* by .... through the park.
4 You can *carry* it wherever you go; that's the great thing about a .... TV.
5 She says she'd *prefer* to stay in and watch TV, but I'm sure she'd .... come out with us.
6 Some of the *popular press* are accused of nasty cheap journalism, but I don't think all the .... are guilty of it.
7 Two of the men *gave themselves up* last night, and the other one .... this morning.
8 The *blast* shook a number of buildings, and there are reports that people heard the .... five miles away.
9 John *arrived* at eight o'clock, but the others didn't .... until nine thirty.
10 You *join* this piece to that piece, then you .... it to the central column.

2

Combine words from the left-hand list with words from the right to form sixteen phrases or compounds.

dish	stainless	fitted	
pain	spare	trade	air
status	pay	background	
stock	public	pulse	
weather	vacuum	food	

forecast	union	fares	
mixer	steel	killer	room
rate	rise	carpet	noise
market	washer	symbol	
opinion	cleaner		

76

— 3 —

Study the picture below for one minute, then close your book and write
down everything you can remember about the room. Give as much detail as
possible. Compare your description with two other partners.

— 4 —

Complete the following sentences with a suitable link word or phrase.

1 He played last night .... his injury.
2 .... he was injured, he still played last night.
3 He scored two goals, which is pretty good .... that he was injured.
4 He scored two goals, which is pretty good .... his injury.
5 The manager won't let him play next week .... he's fully fit.
6 The manager told him he could only play next .... he's fully fit.
7 The manager doesn't want him to play in the midweek game .... he
   makes the injury worse.
8 The manager said he would consider him for the game next Saturday.
   ...., he won't let him play in the midweek game.
9 He desperately wants to play next Saturday, but that will depend, ...,
   on the result of his fitness test on Friday.
10 He is certainly the best player in the team. ...., he has the ability to
   inspire others around him and help them play to their maximum potential.

—— 5

a   The most common sound in English is /ə/:

Example:

mother   about   another   produce   understand   appointment

You will notice that different letters can represent this sound, but it is only on parts of the word that are not stressed:

Example:

☐   ☐   ☐
deliver   advertisement   confused

Mark the main stress on the following words.

ambulance	psychology	necessary	instrument
corruption	emergency	interested	thermometer
presumably	microphone	document	potentially
paragraph	alternative	temperature	machinery

b   ⌷═⌷ Now listen and check your answers.

c   Mark on the words where you think the sound /ə/ appears, compare your answers with a partner, and then listen to the tape again to check.

—— 6

Fill in the gaps in the following text with a suitable word or phrase.

Ambulance crews to step up action

AMBULANCE staff today .... to step up their action in support of an 11 per cent pay ....

They condemned moves to bring in the Army which, said a .... for the health union NUPE, would only lead to a worsening of the situation.

Roger Poole, chief negotiator for the five main .... involved, said: "What is the Government up to?

"Why are they talking about

by Dick Murray

bringing in the Army into a .... which could be settled by ...."

And a spokesman for NUPE .... that ambulance staff could stage sit-ins at stations if the Army was used.

Union .... meet tomorrow to discuss further action but have .... to keep accident and .... services going.

—— 7 ——

Play the following game in groups of four. Choose one verb each from the list below. One person must then start a conversation and use their verb. The next person must then continue the conversation until they have used their verb; and so on. Try to use your verb in different ways, and see how long you can keep the conversation going. Here is your choice of verbs:

get   take   see   leave   keep   catch

—— 8 ——

What could the person be talking about in each of the following sentences?

1 It's cold, damp and draughty.
2 It was quick, simple, and surprisingly painless.
3 It looked very neat and tidy.
4 It's an ingenious thing, and very easy-to-use.
5 It's waterproof and very accurate.
6 It's getting very old and rusty.
7 I fiddled with the knobs but it still kept flickering.
8 I bent it trying to get the top off.
9 You should keep it in the cellar and try to avoid too much vibration.
10 It sleeps about four people but I'm not sure if it's waterproof.

—— 9 ——

Write definitions/explanations of the following words. When you have finished, read your answers to a partner and see if they can tell you the word you are defining.

thermometer   stapler   microscope   stock market   loft
basement   telescope   microphone   wardrobe

—— 10 ——

Complete the missing parts of the following sentences and then compare your answers with a partner.

1 He agreed .... homework.
2 She encouraged .... the money.
3 He let .... his car.
4 I'm thinking .... holiday.
5 She suggested .... with them.
6 I regret .... sixteen.
7 He insisted .... meal.
8 I'm used .... o'clock.
9 I don't remember .... desk.
10 I'm looking forward .... spring.

—— 11 ——

a Discuss the following questions in groups and write down your answers (you will probably need bilingual dictionaries to help you).

1 What facilities would you expect to find in a five-star hotel that you wouldn't find in a two-star hotel?
2 What insects would you expect to see in a hot climate that would not be very common in a cold climate?
3 What tools would you need to change the wheel on a car?
4 What equipment would you consider to be essential for a successful camping holiday?
5 What equipment would you expect to find in a doctor's surgery?
6 What crops would you expect to see on a Japanese farm?
7 What goods would you expect people to try and smuggle through customs?
8 Write down one of your own personal belongings that you would hate to lose.

b Compare your answers with another group, and see if they can identify the people who chose each of the objects in your answer to question 8.

—— 12 ——

This game uses pronunciation to revise a wide range of vocabulary, and can be played with any number of people. Choose a sound and then write as many examples as possible under the headings in this table.

Example:
/æ/ as in cat or /eɪ/ as in late

Living things	Verbs	Places/Things
cat	ran	bank
actor	stand	van
bat	sat	sand
passenger	drank	lap
manager	cancel	ladder

You should do this individually without showing your words to anyone else. You then take it in turns to make up sentences using one word from each column.

Examples:
The cat sat on my lap.
The actor wanted to stand on the ladder.
The manager ran towards the van.

19 Customs

——— 1 ———

a Discuss the following statements in groups, and decide if they are true, false, or impossible to generalize.

In Britain . . .	True/False/Impossible to generalize
1 It is customary to shake hands when you are first introduced to someone.	
2 It is fairly common to shake hands with colleagues at work every morning.	
3 It is very rare for English people to shake hands with children.	
4 English people rarely kiss friends as a form of social greeting.	
5 You would normally address someone as 'sir' or 'madam' if you didn't know their name.	
6 People tend to say their surname first when answering the phone at home.	
7 It is considered rude to ask someone how much they earn.	
8 It is considered bad manners to blow your nose in public.	
9 Most people tend to say 'good morning' or 'good afternoon' to the shop assistant when they are served.	
10 In a restaurant it is customary to attract the waiter's attention by calling out 'waiter'.	

b Now listen to a group of English people discussing these statements, and compare their answers with your own.

c In groups, discuss these statements with reference to your own country or countries.

—— **2** ————————————————————

a Put the following words in the correct circle below. Some words may go
in both circles.

bride   ceremony   church   burial   undertaker   ring
reception   aisle   ashes   groom   vicar   priest   coffin
cemetery   cremation   grave   bridesmaid   wreath
honeymoon   service   best man   registry office   bouquet

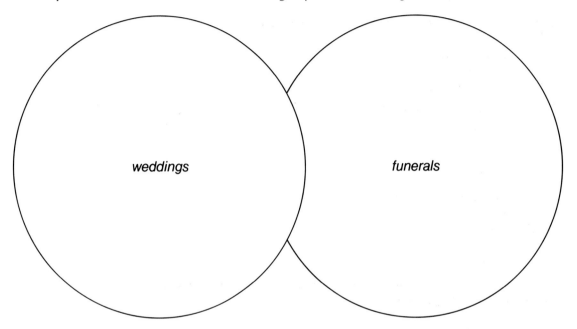

weddings   funerals

b Now reorganize the words under the following headings.

People	Events	Places	Things

c Answer the following questions and then compare your answers in groups.

1 In your religion/country, do weddings take place:
   a) in a church?
   b) at a shrine?
   c) at home?
   d) at a hotel?
   e) in a registry office

2 In your religion/country, do you have a reception after the wedding? If so, who pays for it? Is it:
   a) the bridegroom?
   b) the bride's father?
   c) both sets of parents?

3 At a church wedding, the bride usually walks up the aisle at the beginning of the ceremony:
   a) alone?
   b) with the bridegroom?
   c) with her father?

4 Who keeps the ring during the ceremony? Is it:
   a) the bride?
   b) the bridegroom?
   c) the best man?
   d) the vicar/priest?

5 To get married in your religion/country, do you have to have a religious ceremony and a civic ceremony?

6 Where is Karl Marx buried? In:
   a) Moscow?
   b) Leningrad?
   c) London?
   d) Vienna?

7 In fiction, who rises from his coffin after dark?

8 In your country/religion, what happens to the ashes after someone has been cremated?

———— **3** ————————————————————

a How would you prepare the following foods in your country? Complete the grid and then compare your answers in groups. Use a dictionary to help you.

Method / Food	fry	grill	boil	bake	steam	eat raw
prawns/shrimps						
crab						
mussels						
squid						
kidney						
liver						
peppers						
celery						
cabbage						
cucumber						

b Read through the following recipes. In groups, try and decide which
country they might come from, and which one you would most like to try.

1 Sauté onions, garlic, tomatoes and hot chilli peppers for five minutes, then stir in the lime or lemon juice and add the chicken pieces. Cook until tender. Leave until cool and then chop the meat and strain the vegetables through a sieve. Combine the liquid from the vegetables with almonds, dried shrimp and coconut milk and simmer for fifteen minutes. Add rice flour, the chicken pieces and palm oil. Cook for a further ten minutes.

2 Cut the crab shell into large pieces. Then fry black beans, garlic, ginger and spring onions very quickly before adding minced pork. Fry again for one minute and then add the crab pieces, half a pint of chicken stock or water, and a little dry sherry or rice wine. Heat for ten minutes and then add two beaten eggs. Stir slowly for one minute and then serve.

3 In a large frying pan, sauté the onions and peppers until lightly browned and then add the tomatoes. After several minutes add the pieces of white fish and the squid and cook for a further five minutes. Then add the prawns and mussels and cook for another five minutes. Finally, add the mixture of garlic, parsley and saffron, plus one pint of water, and bring to the boil. Put in the rice and leave it to cook. Remove from the heat and set aside for five minutes before serving.

4 Fry the pieces of liver and kidney with the spring onions and parsley for about five minutes. Then add it to the tripe which has been simmering for twenty minutes. Cook for a further twenty minutes and then strain the liquid and boil the rice in it until cooked. Then whisk the egg yolks with lemon juice and add a few tablespoons of soup, stirring constantly. Pour the mixture back into the soup and add the offal. Heat up again and add a little milk before serving.

SELF-STUDY ACTIVITIES

1 It is a custom in England to use certain words and phrases in particular situations. For your next lesson, find out when the following phrases would be used.

once upon a time   cheers   bless you   say cheese
good luck   congratulations   I beg your pardon
I beg your pardon?   hear hear!   many happy returns

2 There is also a custom for people to make a New Year's resolution on 1 January. This is a decision to do something or to stop doing something in the coming year. Complete the following resolutions (about yourself) and compare them with other members of the class in a future lesson.

a) I'm going to give up . . .
b) I'm going to cut down on . . .
c) I'm going to be . . .
d) I'm going to spend more time . . .
e) I'm going to stop being . . .
f) I'm going to remember to . . .
g) I'm going to improve . . .
h) I'm going to get more . . .

3 For your next lesson, find out the special name given to the following dates in England, and why they are significant.

14 February   1 April   the Friday before Easter   31 October   5 November
24 December   25 December   26 December   31 December

20 Multi-word units

This unit will concentrate on common idiomatic expressions and phrasal verbs. The first exercise also examines ways of learning words on your own through reading texts.

—— 1 ——

a Read through the following text and tick (✓) the numbers which describe what you do when you are reading a text in English.

1 When I meet a new word in a text I usually look up the meaning in a bilingual dictionary and then I carry on reading.
2 When I come across a new word in a reading passage I usually look up the meaning in a monolingual dictionary and then I carry on reading.
3 When I come across a new word in a text I invariably look up the meaning in a dictionary, and then I normally write it down in my notebook before I go on with the text.
4 When I come across a new word in a text I try to work out the meaning from the context and then I carry on reading.
5 When I come across a new word I usually try to figure out the meaning from the context, and then I check in a dictionary to see if I'm right.
6 I invariably look up the meaning first, then I go back to the text to see if the translation or definition in English makes sense in the context.
7 Normally I can't be bothered to look up new words. I skip them and just hope I'll still be able to get the gist of the passage.
8 I reckon it's a waste of time looking up new words. It spoils the enjoyment of reading, and in any case, you never remember them.
9 I've got my own strategy for dealing with new words which is slightly different. I . . .

b While you were reading you probably came across some new words. Did you follow the strategies that you ticked in **a**? Discuss in groups.

c Choose a strategy that you did not tick in **a**, and use it in the following text. When you have finished, discuss your reactions in groups.

A: Where have you been?
B: I've just been to see Yvette and her mother off.
A: Oh? I didn't think they were leaving today.
B: No, originally they weren't, but it's been such a dreadful week that they decided to go home early.
A: How d'you mean, dreadful?
B: Well, Yvette's mother tripped over and hurt her leg; she's been limping around the last couple of days. And Yvette has been feeling absolutely lousy

ever since they arrived – I think she must have picked up a bug or something.

A: Oh dear, what a shame. And not helped by the weather, either.

B: No, it's been appalling. It poured with rain when they went on their river excursion, and yesterday they got soaked on three separate occasions.

A: And you took them to the station, then?

B: Well, I hadn't planned to, but they got held up for ages trying to fix up their tickets, so I picked them up at the travel agency, took them back to the hotel, and then gave them a lift to the station.

A: Oh, I'm sorry I didn't see them before they left.

B: Yes, they were very sorry about that. Anyway, they send their love, and they said they'd be in touch as soon as they get home.

—— 2 ——

a Find the logical ending for each of the sentences beginning on the left. You can use a dictionary to help you.

1 I tried it on . . .	a) but it didn't work very well.
2 I had to put it off . . .	b) because I was starting to cough a lot.
3 He told me to put it out . . .	c) but it didn't fit very well.
4 I had to look it up . . .	d) without a calculator.
5 She told me to pick it up at four . . .	e) because the money wasn't good enough.
6 We tried it out . . .	f) but I couldn't find an ashtray.
7 In the end I had to sort it out . . .	g) but it still wasn't ready when I got there.
8 I just couldn't work it out . . .	h) because I was so busy.
9 I'm getting over it now . . .	i) but it's still a bit untidy.
10 I gave it up last year . . .	j) I'm trying to concentrate.
11 In the end I turned it down . . .	k) but I still feel a bit weak.
12 Could you turn it down a bit . . .?	l) because I didn't understand the meaning.

b Work with a partner and decide what *it* might be in each of the sentences above.

c Write a logical reply to each of the following statements or questions, using one of the verbs from **a** in each of your answers. Work with a partner and then practise the dialogues with a different partner.

Example:
    A: That's a nice blouse.
    B: Yes, would you like to try it on?

1 Is that cigarette still burning?
2 What does this word mean?
3 Don't you eat meat any longer?
4 Did they offer you the job?
5 Is this music too loud?
6 I'd like to help but I'm afraid I've got a dental appointment.
7 The books are in a terrible mess.
8 We can get the picture developed in 24 hours.
9 What did you make the answer to that question?
10 Is she still upset about her exam results?
11 This new scheme will never work.

d Why is the verb *get over (something)* different from the rest of the verbs?

———— 3 ————

a   Phrasal verbs often have more than one meaning, e.g. *pick up* in exercise
1c, so you must be careful when you look up a phrasal verb in a dictionary.
Match the meaning of the verbs in the following contexts with the correct
dictionary definition below.

1 . . . three days ago, but I hope it *turns up* soon otherwise . . .
2 . . . to *turn* it *up* so I could hear the news about . . .
3 . . . but I couldn't *get through*. The operator told me that . . .
4 . . . takes it again, she should *get through* as long as . . .
5 . . . but it didn't *go off* so I overslept. I hope you haven't . . .
6 . . . but I've *gone off* it recently because it gives me . . .
7 . . . because it's only *held up* by a couple of pieces of wood. I think . . .
8 . . . but I was *held up* for ages at the airport because . . .

get through. 1 If you **get through** something such   PHRASAL VB : V +
as a task, you complete it, especially when it re-   PREP, HAS PASS
quires a lot of effort. EG *It is difficult to get through*   = wade
this amount of work in such a short time... We tried   through
to get through the whole play in two hours.
2 If you **get through** a period of time during which   PHRASAL VB : V +
something unpleasant is happening, you manage to   PREP, HAS PASS
live through it. EG *They helped me to get through that*   = survive
time... How do John and Sylvia ever get through
Minnesota winters?
3 If you **get through** a large amount of something,   PHRASAL VB : V +
you completely use it up. EG *He had got through all*   PREP, HAS PASS
his money... I got through about six pounds worth of   = run through
drink.
4 If you **get through** to someone, **4.1** you succeed in   PHRASAL VB : V +
making them understand something that you are   ADV + *to*
trying to tell them. EG *Howard, how do I get through*   ⇑ reach
to you? **4.2** you succeed in contacting them on the   = get
telephone. EG *I finally got through at twenty past ten.*   PHRASAL VB : V +
5 If you **get through** or get through an examination,   ADV
you pass it. EG *They haven't got a chance of getting*   PHRASAL VB : V +
through... He qualifies if he gets through his two   ADV/PREP
subjects this year.   ⇑ succeed
6 If a law or proposal **gets through,** it is officially   PHRASAL VB :
approved by something such as a parliament or   V-ERG + ADV/
committee. EG *If this new White Paper gets through,*   PREP
there will be no subsidized meals... The bill might not   = go through
have been able to get through Congress.

turn up 1 If someone or something **turns up,** they   PHRASAL VB : V +
arrive somewhere or appear, often unexpectedly; a   ADV
fairly informal use. EG *He turned up at rehearsal the*   = show up
next day looking awful.
2 If something **turns up** or is turned up, it is found,   PHRASAL VB :
discovered, or noticed; a fairly informal use. EG *The*   V-ERG + ADV
missing book turned up three weeks later in the
stationery cupboard... You must be willing to take a
job as soon as one turns up... If I turn up anything,
you'll be the first to know.
3 When you **turn up** something such as a radio or   PHRASAL VB : V +
heater, you increase the amount of sound or heat   O + ADV
being produced, by adjusting the controls. EG *Turn*   ≠ turn down
the volume control up... Could you turn the fire up?
4 When someone **turns up** a dress, skirt, pair of   PHRASAL VB : V +
trousers, etc, they fold up the bottom and stitch it in   O + ADV
place to shorten it or make a hem.   ⇑ alter
   ≠ let down

hold up. 1 If you **hold up** your hand or something   PHRASAL VB : V +
you have in your hand, you move it upwards into a   O + ADV
particular position and keep it there. EG *Ralph held*   ⇑ raise
up his hand. 'Why shouldn't we get our own?' he   = lift
asked... The Englishman held up the rifle.
2 If one thing **holds up** another, it is placed under the   PHRASAL VB : V +
other thing in order to support it and prevent it from   O + ADV
falling. EG *There were tremendous pillars holding up*   = prop up
high ceilings... These books hold the bed up.
3 If something or someone **holds** you **up,** they delay   PHRASAL VB : V +
you or make you late. EG *The whole thing was held*   O + ADV
up about half an hour... These slogans persuaded her   = detain
to hold up the procession.
4 If someone **holds** you **up,** they point a weapon at   PHRASAL VB : V +
you in order to make you give them money or   O + ADV
valuables. EG *He held me up at the point of a gun...*   = rob
Banks were held up with pistols and sawn-off shot-
guns.

go off. 1 If you **go off** somewhere, you leave a place,   PHRASAL VB : V +
usually in order to do something. EG *He had gone off*   ADV, USU + A
to work... She went off to look at the flowers.
2 If you **go off** someone or something, you stop liking   PHRASAL VB :
them; an informal use. EG *He's gone off the idea... I*   ORDER V + ADV +
think she's going off him a bit.   O
3 If you **go off,** you fall asleep; an informal use. EG *He*   PHRASAL VB : V +
went off as soon as his head touched the pillow.   ADV
4 If something **goes off, 4.1** it explodes. EG *I could*   PHRASAL VB : V +
hear the bombs going off on the other side of the   ADV
city. **4.2** it makes a sudden loud noise. EG *The alarm*   PHRASAL VB : V +
went off but he tried to ignore it. **4.3** it stops   ADV
operating. EG *The light only goes off at night.*   PHRASAL VB : V +
   ADV
5 If an organized event **goes off** in a particular way,   PHRASAL VB : V +
it takes place in that way. EG *The meeting went off*   ADV + A
well.   = go
6 Food or drink that has **gone off** has become stale,   PHRASAL VB : V +
sour, or rotten.   ADV

b   Write a suitable beginning for each of the contexts above while a partner finishes each of them in an appropriate way. When you have finished, read the complete contexts to see if they make sense.

Example:
   . . . three days ago, but I hope it turns up soon otherwise . . .

   I lost my book three days ago, but I hope it turns up soon otherwise I'll have to buy a new one.

c   Would you say the different meanings are connected in any way or are they totally unrelated? If they are unrelated, is that true for *all* of the dictionary meanings for that verb? Discuss with a partner.

——— **4** ———————————————————————————

a   We often confirm statements or questions by repeating the information through different words with the same meaning.

Example:
   A: He rejected your offer, then?
   B: Yeah, he turned it down.

Respond to the following questions using the verbs and phrases in the box in your answers.

get hold of (someone)	split up	keep an eye on
off the beaten track	set off	get on one's nerves
get by	tear (something) to pieces	get a move on
hang on	get rid of (something)	take it in turns

 1 Do you want me to wait?
 2 I find her very irritating, don't you?
 3 It's a bit of a remote place, isn't it?
 4 You can manage on £100 a week, then?
 5 Shall we throw out these old cushions, then?
 6 They left for Scotland quite early, didn't they?
 7 They separated a while ago, didn't they?
 8 You didn't manage to contact him, then?
 9 The critics really hated the film, didn't they?
10 You want me to look after these suitcases for a while?
11 D'you alternate if you both want to use the car?
12 Are you trying to tell me to hurry up?

b   Practise the dialogues in pairs.

SELF-STUDY ACTIVITIES

1 What extra information is being provided by the phrases in brackets in the following sentences?

Example:
   I met her last night (by chance).
   The phrase 'by chance' tells us that the meeting wasn't planned.

   a) I know him (by sight).
   b) I'll give it to you tomorrow (without fail).
   c) Could you send it to me (by return of post)?
   d) There were about thirty of them (at a guess).
   e) I don't know the answer (off-hand).
   f) They've gone to America (for good).
   g) I gave him my cassettes (in return).
   h) Let's go to the theatre (for a change).

2 Some words are found together so often that you should learn them as phrases. Which words on the left often go with the words on the right?

vast	utter	bone	stiff	chaos	alone
narrow	bored	fast	escape	headache	majority
wide	thick	all	range	asleep	coincidence
sheer	dire	splitting	trouble	idle	fog

'It's marvellous when you come to think about it – thanks to satellites, most of Europe is being bored stiff by this programme . . .'

3 Choose three or four phrasal verbs or phrases from this unit and build them into a little story. When you have finished you can repeat the activity for a different group of verbs or phrases.

Example:
   The village was a bit *off the beaten track* so we *set off* quite early. We *took it in turns* to drive and finally got there around lunchtime. It wasn't our lucky day though, because it *poured with rain* all afternoon.

21 Men and women

1

a Complete the following sentences with statements you believe to be true. Use a dictionary if necessary.

1 In my experience men are (much) .... than women.
2 Women, on the other hand, tend to be more .... than men.
3 Men are often obsessed with ....
4 Women are inclined to be more aware of .... than men.
5 Unlike men, women ....
6 The most irritating thing about men/women is that they ....
7 Compared with men/women, women/men ....
8 One thing that men and women both have in common is that ....

b In groups, read your sentences to each other and discuss the answers.

c The picture on the right shows one view of the male brain. In groups (men in one group and women in the other), produce your view of the female brain and then compare your answers.

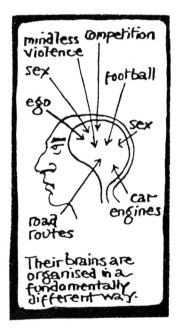

mindless violence
competition
sex
football
ego
sex
car engines
road routes

Their brains are organised in a fundamentally different way.

—— 2 ——

a Read through the following questions. Use a dictionary if necessary.

	Letter (A–L)
1 What does your husband/wife do for a living?	
2 Does he/she mind you working full-time?	
3 Are you likely to have to move because of your husband's/wife's job?	G
4 Have you got any children?	
5 Are you planning to start a family?	
6 Who looks after the children while you're at work?	
7 Who would take time off work if the children were ill?	
8 Are you willing to give up weekends to work overtime?	
9 Promotion could involve moving to a different area. Would you be prepared to move?	
10 The job is very stressful. Do you feel you're good at coping with stress?	
11 How do you feel about working in a job where most of your colleagues will be of the opposite sex?	
12 If you were offered the job, would you be prepared to make a commitment to the company for at least three years?	

b 🔲 You are going to hear answers to the above questions, but not in the same order. As you listen, put the correct letter (A–L) beside each question. One answer has already been done for you.

c According to a recent survey, women are often asked more personal questions at job interviews than men. In groups, discuss the questions above. Would they be asked of a man, a woman, or both? Do you think some of these questions should not be asked at all?

—— 3 ——

a Do you associate the words in this list with men, women, or both? Make three lists and be prepared to explain your groupings. Use a dictionary if necessary.

poetry	riot	sensitivity	comradeship	betrayal	mood
butcher	rape	flattery	gang	envy	poverty	politics
friendship	anger	cruelty	oppression	hypocrisy	religion
violence	compassion	suffering	birth	care	loyal

b Discuss your answers in groups.

c We often remember words by forming associations: a word has a connection with a second word, and the second word is associated with a third word, and so on.

Example:

    sheep→wool→jumper→knitting→mother→childhood→**birthdays**

or

    sheep→lamb→vegetables→earth→worm→silk→**blouse**

Form associations between the following pairs using words from the list in **a**.

envy .... **gang**
butcher .... **poetry**
riot .... **birth**

d Now form your own word chain using as many words from the list on the previous page as possible. You can also add your own words.

—— **4** ————————————————————————————

a Are the following sentences about men or women? Complete them using suitable male or female words, e.g. he/she, his/her, men/women, boys/girls. Are there any sentences which could be either?

1 .... took off the pink nylon dressing gown and threw it on the floor.
2 As the midday heat grew more intense, beads of sweat ran down the tanned weather-beaten face, but .... carried on digging.
3 .... paced nervously up and down the corridor until the nurse appeared.
4 .... decided the brooch wasn't quite right so .... took it off.
5 .... had often been teased for .... angelic looks and long blond hair.
6 The bushy eyebrows and wide nostrils gave .... a fierce, almost threatening appearance.
7 As the comments grew louder both .... blushed and started to giggle.
8 Whether it was a new car, the latest hi-fi, a camera or whatever, ... could never resist the temptation to show off .... wealth.
9 .... put .... hands on .... hips and smiled.
10 With both hands in .... pockets, ... strolled down the road whistling .... favourite tune.
11 The old slippers and wrinkled brown tights only added to the comic effect, as .... stood on the doorstep and waved frantically.
12 .... carefully ironed the sleeves and then folded the shirt and put it straight into the suitcase. One more, ... thought, and then .... could join the lads down the pub.
13 .... slipped the bag off .... shoulder, swept .... hair back gracefully, and then glanced at the table opposite.
14 Despite the teacher's angry look, ... continued to slouch in .... chair, with both feet resting defiantly on the desk in front.
15 .... had a long slender neck and skin that was white as snow.

b Compare and discuss your answers.

SELF-STUDY ACTIVITIES

---

1 Find the missing word in each of the following pairs.

Example: male / *female*

a) .... / feminine   h) monk / ....
b) nephew / ....   i)   .... / convent
c) actor / ....   j)   headmaster / ....
d) .... / bride   k) .... / cow
e) host / ....   l)   .... / hen
f) widower / ....   m) hero / ....
g) waiter / ....   n) .... / landlady

2 Write down twenty words which you only associate with men or women.
These words may be items of clothing, physical characteristics, personal
qualities, etc. Compare your answers with other members of class in the next
lesson.

22 Ways of saying things

a We can make requests in different ways, and our choice of language will depend on, among other factors:

– the relationship between speaker and listener;
– how certain we are of a positive response to our request.

Choose the most suitable request for each of the following situations and then discuss your answers with a partner.

1 Talking to a waiter in a restaurant:
   a) Excuse me. Where's the toilet?
   b) Excuse me. Do you happen to know where the toilet is?

2 To a fellow passenger at an airport:
   a) Keep an eye on my suitcase, will you?
   b) Do you think you could possibly keep an eye on my suitcase for a minute?

3 To a friend at work:
   a) Have you got a minute?
   b) Do you think I could possibly have a quick word with you?

4 To a fellow passenger on a train:
   a) OK if I open the window?
   b) Do you mind if I open the window?

5 To a close friend:
   a) Could you lend me 50p?
   b) I was wondering if you could possibly lend me 50p?

6 To a fellow traveller on a train:
   a) Give me a hand with this case, will you?
   b) Sorry to trouble you, but do you think you could give me a hand with this case?

7 To the landlady in an English home (this is the second day in their house):
   a) OK if I use the phone?
   b) Do you think I could possibly use your phone?

8 To the same landlady on the third day of your stay:
   a) I doubt if I'll be home for dinner. Is that OK?
   b) Would you mind very much if I didn't come back for dinner?

b With a partner, think of a context in which the remaining eight requests would be suitable.

c   Here are eight replies. Match the replies with the above requests, and decide if the reply could be used with both requests in each situation or just one of them.

1   Yeah OK, but don't be long.
2   No, no, go ahead.
3   Sure. Where do you want it?
4   I'm sorry, I haven't the faintest idea.
5   No, no problem at all.
6   Well actually, I'm a bit tied up at the moment.
7   I'm afraid I haven't got any cash on me at the moment.
8   Yes of course. Help yourself.

d   Practise similar conversations with a partner, and bring each one to a logical conclusion.

Example:

   A: Excuse me. Do you happen to know where Bond Street is?
   B: No I'm sorry, I haven't the faintest idea.
   A: OK never mind. Thanks anyway.

──── 2 ────

a   Can you think of a more informal (colloquial) word or phrase which could be used in place of the underlined words in the following sentences?

1   There's no hurry; we've got <u>plenty</u> of time.
2   When will dinner be ready? I'm <u>really hungry</u>.
3   The flat's next to the underground which is very <u>convenient</u> for work.
4   The <u>children</u> will be going back to school next week.
5   Word processing may seem difficult at first but <u>as soon as you understand how to do it</u>, it's easy.
6   Hey, someone has <u>stolen</u> my dictionary.
7   The others liked the film but I thought it was <u>boring</u>.
8   <u>I'm sure</u> you'll be pleased when the conference is over.
9   <u>What's the matter?</u>
10   We really need a company with <u>expertise</u> for this contract.
11   It's not an easy exam but I <u>think</u> she'll pass.
12   <u>Would you like a snack</u> before we go out?

b   Listen to the answers on the tape and write down any words or phrases which are different from your own answers.

c   Write twelve sentences of your own, with each one including one of the words or phrases from above. When you have finished, move round the class and read one of your sentences to each student. When you read your sentences 'cough' in place of the word or phrase from above: can your partner supply the correct missing word?

—— **3** ——

a   Two people can witness the same event but interpret it in different ways. Often, our choice of vocabulary will reflect our attitude to the event:

Example:
    This is how two people judge a new colleague at work:

    A: His youth and enthusiasm are great assets to the company.
    B: His inexperience and naivety are real weaknesses.

Choose one of the words or phrases in each case to complete the following texts.

1 | Trouble / Problems | started / flared up | when a | group / gang | of | rowdy / noisy | youths / demonstrators / thugs |

charged / pushed towards | the police, who were lined up outside the embassy.

They | defended themselves / retaliated | with | sticks / riot shields | and within minutes there

was | quite a disturbance / a running battle | around the square. We have reports that some of

the | leading troublemakers / demonstrators | have been arrested, and that | several / a number of |

police officers have received | nasty head wounds. / facial injuries.

2   It's a | cramped / cosy | little cottage, | with many original features. / badly in need of modernization. |

At the back there is a completely | overgrown / unspoilt | garden, and a | small stream / smelly ditch |

running along the bottom. | To make matters worse, / What's more, | it's in

| the middle of nowhere, / a quiet peaceful setting, | but / and | within easy reach of / miles from | West Lynn, which

| now attracts a number of overseas visitors / is now packed with foreign tourists | in the summer and has become

| a busy, thriving centre. / almost unbearable.

b   Read your texts to a partner and discuss the differences.

—— **4** ————————————————————————

a Read the following poem, look up any new words in a dictionary, and
then answer the question below.

Aphasia

I'm seven and I'm dead bright,
But words give me a fright.
Words are bullies.
Sneaky things. They gabble and lie.
Sometimes trying to understand
Them makes me cry.
Words hurt. Words are all over the place.
They get shoved in my face.
I don't know why but
Words make me cry.

I wish words were things
You could hug,
Or that they smelt nice.
I wish they came in bottles
Like fizzy-drinks, or melted
Like ice-cream. But they don't.
Words are mean. They bully me.
Lock me away
From what I want to say.

I can't even ask for help,
And I'm only seven
(And a bit).
Words spread nasty gossip.
They must. Otherwise why
Would people think I'm thick?
Words,
They make me sick
Inside.

from *Storm Damage* by Brian Patten

**Write down eight things the poet dislikes about words and then compare
your answers with a partner.**

Example:

  words give him a fright.

b With a partner, think of eight positive things that words can do.

c   **The poet uses similes and metaphor to describe his feelings:**

Example:
  I wish words . . . melted like ice-cream.

Complete the similes below in a suitable (or poetic) way, and then compare your answers with other members of the class.

 1 When she's in the water she floats like . . .
 2 Although it was quite shallow, he sank like . . .
 3 When he walks in those new shoes he squeaks like . . .
 4 The snow covered the mountain top like . . .
 5 When he's hungry he eats like . . .
 6 His socks smell like . . .
 7 When she laughs she sounds like . . .
 8 But when she plays the violin it's like . . .
 9 The crowd were screaming and yelling like . . .
10 By the end of the party the room was like . . .

Confucius at the office

SELF-STUDY ACTIVITIES

---

1 Certain similes have become standard phrases in English. Choose a word
 from the box to complete each of the sentences below.

bone	sheet	post	gold	bat	
hot cakes	log	fox	feather	beetroot	

 a) When I told him the news he went white as a ....
 b) You'll have to speak up, she's deaf as a ....
 c) He shouldn't drive a car because he's blind as a ....
 d) Don't worry about me; I always sleep like a ....
 e) I was amazed when I picked her up; she's light as a ....
 f) We took the children to the restaurant and they were as good as ....
 g) When she made that silly remark she went red as a ....
 h) Our latest product is selling like ....
 i) I'll have to water the plants because the ground is dry as a ....
 j) You'd better watch him because he's as cunning as a ....

2 Every language has its own proverbs and sayings. For your next lesson, find
 out the meaning of the following sayings in English, and whether you have an
 equivalent saying in your own language.

 a) Actions speak louder than words.
 b) Make a mountain out of a molehill.
 c) Let sleeping dogs lie.
 d) A bad workman always blames his tools.
 e) Practice makes perfect.
 f) Familiarity breeds contempt.
 g) The grass is always greener on
  the other side.
 h) Two wrongs don't make a right.

3 In exercise **2** of this unit you learned one meaning of the words below. Can
 you write sentences to show them being used with different meanings?

 load   starve   handy   pinch   drag   bet

23 Ideas and opinions

a The following diagram shows the possible development of a plan or idea. Work through the diagram and then complete it using the phrases from the box. Use a dictionary to help you if necessary.

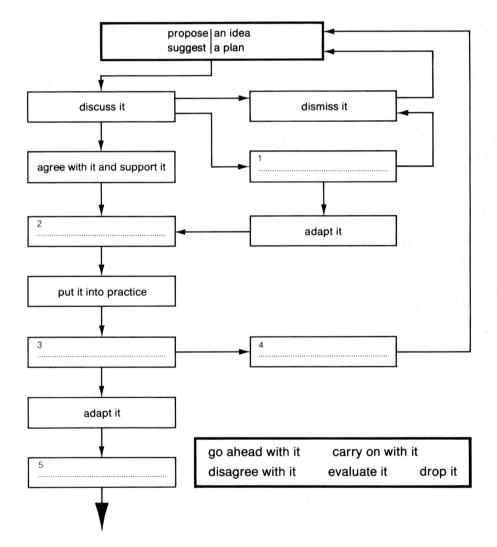

b Find synonyms from the diagram for the following words.

reject   give up   scheme   amend   put forward   assess

>>>→

c Work in groups of five and sit in a circle. Follow these instructions carefully.

1 Choose one suggestion each from the following list and write it down at the top of a blank piece of paper.
   a) Students should sit next to a different person each lesson.
   b) Students should pay a fine if they speak their language during an English lesson.
   c) Lessons should be longer and with fewer breaks.
   d) Students who are late shouldn't be allowed into class.
   e) The desks/chairs should be arranged in a different way.

2 Pass your piece of paper to the person on your left. On the paper in front of you, write down a reason why you support this idea and then pass the paper to the person on your left.

3 On your piece of paper, write down a reason why you disagree with the idea, and then pass the paper to the person on your left.

4 On your piece of paper, amend the original proposal in such a way that everyone might agree with it. Pass it to the person on your left.

5 You now have the piece of paper you started with, and it is your decision what to do next. Would you like to go ahead with the amended proposal or would you reject it?

d Tell the others in the group about your idea and your decision. If you have decided to go ahead with any of the proposals, discuss the possible problems of putting them into practice, and how you would evaluate the schemes.

—— 2 ——

a Read the following text about the ways that different cities and countries are trying to solve the problem of traffic congestion. Use a dictionary to help you if necessary.

- In **Tokyo**, cars must prove that they have access to off-street parking before being allowed into the city.
- In **Stockholm**, cars will soon need a toll card which reduces in value each time the car enters the city centre. The card doubles as a season ticket giving free use of public transport.
- **Denmark**, which has no car industry, imposes heavy taxes on all imported cars. This approach could be used by other countries, simply by taxing all cars heavily.

- In **Paris**, 200,000 central parking spaces are being removed to deter motorists.
- **Bordeaux** will ban or restrict cars on 75 per cent of its streets in the next ten years.
- **Freiburg in Germany** has achieved an 18 per cent shift from cars to public transport through an ultra-cheap season ticket for buses and trams.
- **Groningen in Holland** has reduced inner-city congestion by 23 per cent by dividing the city centre into four traffic zones: to get from one zone to another cars must go back out to the ring road and then back in again.
- **Los Angeles** provides financial incentives for employers to set up mini-bus or car-share services for staff. Many freeways now have lanes reserved for these buses and shared cars.
- **Singapore** requires vehicles entering the city centre to buy an extra licence.

b   **What do you think of these ideas? Complete the sentences below (by adding the name of a city or country) which express your views.**

1 The .... scheme sounds attractive but I think it is a bit naive and unrealistic. I doubt if it would work in many places.
2 Personally, I think the .... scheme sounds absolutely ridiculous.
3 I think the .... scheme is by far the most practical.
4 I'm not in favour of the .... scheme because it sounds elitist.
5 I'm very much against the .... scheme because it restricts personal choice and freedom.
6 The .... scheme sounds OK in theory but I'm not sure if it'll work in practice.
7 I think the .... scheme is quite practical but I doubt if it'll really solve the problem in the long term.
8 The .... scheme sounds like a good idea but I'm not sure if people will accept it.

c   **Discuss your answers in groups.**

——— 3 ———————

a Complete the table below and look up the meanings of any new words.

Verb	Noun(s)	Verb	Noun(s)
restrict impose advertise produce reduce warn		deter abuse consume persuade tax smuggle	

b In groups, discuss the following statements. Do you agree or disagree?

1 We should ban all media advertising of alcoholic drinks.
2 We should impose restrictions on media advertising of alcoholic drinks.
3 We should increase the price of alcoholic products in order to deter consumption.
4 Alcoholic drinks should carry warning labels (like cigarettes in many countries).
5 The measures above would reduce the consumption of alcohol.

c Read the following text. Does it agree or disagree with the statements above?

Alcoholic drinks are legitimate products that meet a clearly established and longstanding consumer demand. They generate income, tax revenues and jobs worldwide.

As a manufacturer of high quality products the company has the right to market and promote its goods in a responsible manner.

However, the range of concerns over alcohol has led to calls for restrictions on drinks promotion in order to minimise the alleged adverse effects. Such restrictions will not reach or help problem drinkers, who need to be addressed by more closely targeted education and treatment programmes.

Some people believe that there is a direct relationship between the number of people abusing alcohol and overall alcohol consumption. It is claimed that, by controlling the price and availability of drink and by imposing restrictions on advertising, consumption will be reduced and, consequently, alcohol abuse will decline. But evidence from the marketplace and considerable academic research have consistently failed to demonstrate that a clear relationship between levels of consumption and abuse exists.

In those countries where taxation has been used to increase price and reduce consumption, alcohol abuse still persists. Consumers have often resorted to illicit sources of alcohol, such as moonshine, or smuggled products. In Sweden, for example, where taxation has been used to deter consumption, there has been no discernible reduction in levels of alcohol abuse.

There is no evidence to suggest that the banning of advertising has any discernible effect upon alcohol abuse. In countries where advertising has been banned, consumption is increasing. While in countries where advertising is widespread, alcohol consumption is declining.

The effect of alcohol advertising is not to increase overall consumption, but rather to persuade consumers to select one brand over another.

Some countries believe that drinks should carry warning labels. Again, this is an attempted solution that does not address the problem. Alcohol abusers are unlikely to heed such warnings and would be better served by educational approaches.

d **Alcoholism is a very serious addiction, but most of us have things we are, or could easily become, addicted to. Is this true of anything in the following list? Read through and then discuss your answers in groups. Use a dictionary to help you if necessary.**

shopping	expensive jewellery	card games
keeping fit	collecting things	learning English
jigsaw puzzles	(often that you	new gadgets
spending money	don't need)	not wasting anything
eating sweets	chess	work (such people are
knitting or sewing	crosswords	called workaholics)
dieting	computers	
personal cleanliness	DIY	

--- SELF-STUDY ACTIVITIES ---

1 The following verbs appeared in exercise **1** in this unit. Find the nouns formed from these verbs and complete the table.

Verb	Noun	Verb	Noun
propose		assess	
evaluate		discuss	
suggest		reject	
amend		adapt	
dismiss		agree	

2a The text in exercise **3** contained a number of compound adjectives, for example:

long-standing   worldwide   widespread

Match words from the two lists below to form twelve compound adjectives.

time-	world-	multi-	boiled	national	term
long-	law-	far-	minded	sleeved	abiding
home-	self-	short-	class	heeled	consuming
hard-	high-	narrow-	made	fetched	employed

b Choose nouns from the following list which could partner the adjectives above.

egg   shirt   attitude   job   company   citizen
aim   cakes   story   shoes   player   builder

3 You can keep a record of vocabulary describing important issues using the following grid:

For	Against	Mixed feelings	No opinion
nuclear disarmament	capital punishment	abortion	sex education in schools

Add more issues to the grid and compare it with others in a future lesson.

24 Revision and expansion

—— 1 ——

Replace the underlined words in the following sentences with a more specific word, i.e. a more specific way of looking, walking, and so on.

Example:
  When I was in the army we often had to ~~walk~~ *march* twenty miles a day.

1 He's been <u>walking</u> like that ever since his accident.
2 We were just <u>walking</u> along the beach when we heard the scream.
3 He was so impatient he kept <u>walking</u> up and down the platform until the train arrived.
4 I <u>looked</u> at my watch and realized it was time to go.
5 It made me feel very uncomfortable the way they kept <u>looking</u> at us.
6 She <u>said</u> something but I couldn't hear what it was.
7 Once they start <u>laughing</u>, I'm afraid they can't stop.
8 I could see three boys <u>sitting</u> at the back. They looked bored stiff.

—— 2 ——

a Complete the following short dialogues.

A: Do you happen . . .?
B: No sorry, I haven't the . . .

A: I was . . .?
B: Yeah, provided you . . .

A: D'you fancy . . .?
B: Well actually, I'm . . .

A: Would you . . .?
B: No, go . . .

A: D'you think I could . . .?
B: Yeah hang on, I'll . . .

b Practise the dialogues in pairs, bringing each conversation to a natural end.

3

a Find ten pairs of synonyms in the list below.

think   kids   employ   take on   tied up
manage   arrange   delayed   fix up   know-how
extinguish   children   held up   get over   expertise
reckon   recover   busy   get by   put out

b With a partner, explain the difference between each pair of synonyms.

4

a What special names are given to the following dates in English?

1 24 December
2 25 December
3 26 December
4 31 December
5 1 January

*'This saves a lot of time on Christmas
Day. It's already broken.'*

b In groups, tell each other what you eat and do on these days.

5

a Put the words below into the correct column on the right according to
the sound of the underlined letters.

rude   flood   stood   mood
bully   hug   shove   prove
butcher   customary
enthusiastic   root   cushion
dull   cucumber   luxury

/uː/	/ʌ/	/ʊ/
soon	love	book

b  Listen and check your answers.

— 6 —

The words in the box are all connected with clothes and accessories. Can you create six different word groups using these words?

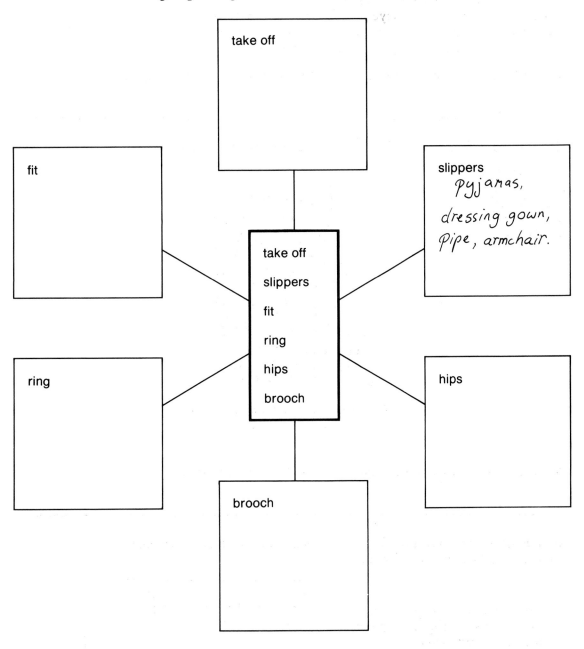

take off

fit

slippers
  *Pyjamas,
dressing gown,
pipe, armchair.*

take off

slippers

fit

ring

hips

brooch

ring

hips

brooch

—— 7 ——

Complete the following sentences and then compare your answers in groups.

1 My mother is inclined to be
.... than me.

2 Unlike my mother, I am
....

3 Compared with my father I am
....

4 One thing I have in common with
my father is that we both
....

5 The best thing about my parents is
that they
....

6 The most irritating thing about my
parents is that they
....

—— 8 ——

a Combine words from the two lists to form common phrases and word
partnerships.

Example:
  whistle a tune

whistle	pour	have	a word	someone a lift	the paper
pay	make	burst	sense	one's nose	time off
fold	be	shake	the instructions	someone's attention	
take	give	blow	with rain	into flames	in touch
follow	attract		a tune	a fine	hands

b Write sentences which include at least two of the combinations in the
same sentence.

Example:

  It is impossible to blow your nose and whistle a tune at the same time.

—— 9 ——

a Organize the words below into words with one syllable and words with two syllables.

suit   yacht   chaos   quite   quiet   react   ruin
reach   naked   shocked   poem   bias   doubt   riot
fares   whereas   suede   client   fuel   queue

b Listen and check your answers.

—— 10 ——

a Respond to the following questions using a more extreme word or phrase than the underlined words. You mustn't use the same word in more than one answer.

Example:
   A: Were you <u>tired</u> when you arrived?
   B: Yes, we were (absolutely) <u>exhausted</u>.

1 Did you get <u>wet</u> last night?
2 Are you <u>hungry</u>?
3 It was a <u>silly</u> thing to say, don't you think?
4 Don't you feel <u>very well</u>?
5 It's been a <u>bad</u> week, hasn't it?
6 The weather was <u>pretty bad</u>, wasn't it?
7 It's <u>full</u> of tourists this time of year, isn't it?
8 The pain was quite <u>bad</u>, wasn't it?

b Practise the dialogues in pairs.

—— 11 ——

Write sentences which illustrate the meaning of the ten items below, and then see if a partner can produce ten more sentences to show them being used with a different meaning.

give up   handy   bet   get through   pick up
turn up   load   go off   turn down   hold up

───── **12** ──────────────────────────────

a Complete the following sentences using the noun formed from the underlined verb or adjective in the sentence.

1 We were very <u>poor</u> when I was a child, but .... is nothing to be ashamed of.
2 Our work is <u>assessed</u> every week, but it's the end of term .... that really counts.
3 I've never <u>criticized</u> her work, but I know she's upset about the .... she's received from other teachers.
4 It may <u>deter</u> people for a while, but in the long term I don't think that .... are the best way to solve the problem.
5 I <u>proposed</u> the idea originally, but it has been amended in so many ways that I don't really feel it's my .... any longer.
6 Some people say she's been <u>disloyal</u>, but personally I've never doubted her ....
7 People of our generation <u>consume</u> less but overall .... is rising.
8 I get <u>angry</u> quite quickly but I don't think .... ever solves anything.

───── **13** ──────────────────────────────

Write one of the following stories and then compare your answer with someone who wrote the other story.

1 A demonstration by a group campaigning against the use of animals in scientific research ends in trouble. You are a journalist for a local paper and you support this cause. Write your report on the demonstration.
2 A demonstration by a group campaigning against the use of animals in scientific research ends in trouble. You are a journalist for a local paper and you believe that people who support this cause are naive and irresponsible. Write your report on the demonstration.

───── **14** ──────────────────────────────

In the last five units, *get* has been used in a number of phrasal verbs and phrases. How many can you remember?

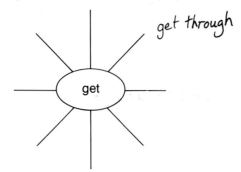

───── 15 ─────────────────────────────

Can you think of words or phrases which could serve as opposites of the following?

upset	birth	yell	off the beaten track
nasty	tied up	spoilt	fizzy
hypocrisy	cramped	surname	feather
gold	condemn	float	

───── 16 ─────────────────────────────

a   Complete the following network and extend it.

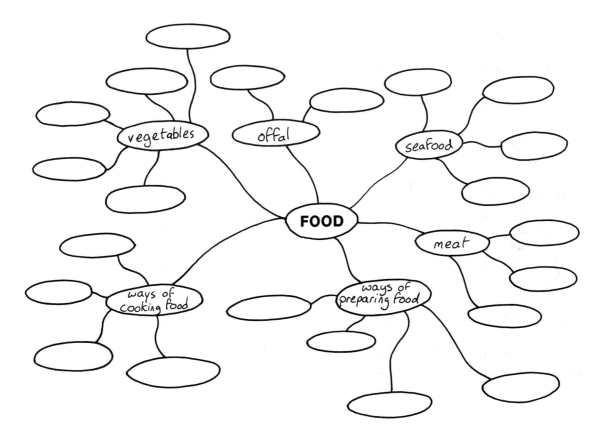

b   Produce your own network about marriage or death and then compare your answers in groups.

Word-building tables

Building new words from the 'root' form is an important part of vocabulary expansion. For example, to the verb *improve* we can add the suffix *-ment* to form the noun *improvement*; to the noun *music* we can add *-al* and form the adjective *musical*. Sometimes there will be a small change in spelling, e.g. the noun from *promote* is *promotion* (and not *promoteion*).

There are no clear rules about the use of suffixes in word building but some suffixes are very common and you can sometimes guess the correct suffix to build a new word. Here are some common examples – see how many words you can think of with these suffixes and then check your words in the tables on the following pages.

Noun (abstract)	Noun (personal)	Adjective	Verb
-tion	-er	-able	-ise (-ize)
-sion	-or	-ive	
-ment	-ist	-ent	
-ness		-al	
-ence		-ic	
-ance		-ous	
-ism		-y	
-y			
-ity			

Spaces have been left where there is no derived word, or where the derived word is extremely uncommon.

TABLE 1: General noun + personal noun + adjective + verb

General noun	Personal noun	Adjective	Verb
addiction	addict	addictive	–
advertising/ advertisement	advertiser	–	advertise
advice	adviser	advisory	advise
accusation	(the) accused	accusatory	accuse
alcohol/alcoholism	alcoholic	alcoholic	–
amateurism	amateur	amateurish	–
athletics	athlete	athletic	–
begging	beggar	–	beg
conformity	conformist	–	conform
consumption	consumer	consuming	consume
contribution	contributor	contributory	contribute
cowardice	coward	cowardly	–
creativity	creator	(un)creative	create
crime	criminal	criminal	–
criticism	critic	critical (of)	criticise
cynicism	cynic	cynical	–
death	(the) deceased	dead/deadly/deathly	die
democracy	democrat	(un)democratic	democratise
demonstration	demonstrator	demonstrative/ demonstrable	demonstrate
dictatorship	dictator	dictatorial	dictate
drama	dramatist	dramatic	dramatise
economy/economics	economist	(un)economic/al	economise
employment	employer/ employee	(un)employed	employ
execution	executioner	–	execute
expertise	expert	expert	–
foolishness	fool	foolish	–
friendship	friend	friendly	befriend
growth	grower	growing	grow
hypocrisy	hypocrite	hypocritical	–
illustration	illustrator	illustrative	illustrate
interpretation	interpreter	interpretative	interpret
judgement	judge	judicial	judge
management	manager	managerial	manage
music	musician	musical	(compose)
negotiation	negotiator	(non)negotiable	negotiate
origin/originality	originator	original	originate
oppression	oppressor	oppressive	oppress
optimism	optimist	optimistic	–
pessimism	pessimist	pessimistic	–
poetry/poem	poet	poetic	–
politics	politician	political	politicise
practice	practitioner	(im)practical	practise

(Table 1 continued)

General noun	Personal noun	Adjective	Verb
production/ productivity/produce	producer	(un)productive	produce
professionalism	professional	(un)professional	–
profit	profiteer	(un)profitable	profit
psychology	psychologist	psychological	–
rape	rapist	–	rape
science	scientist	(un)scientific	–
strangulation	strangler	–	strangle
supervision	supervisor	supervisory	supervise
surgery	surgeon	surgical	(operate (on))
training	trainer/trainee	(un)trained	train

TABLE 2: Noun + adjective + verb

Noun	Adjective	Verb
adaptation	(un)adaptable	adapt
adjustment	(un)adjustable	adjust
admission	(in)admissible	admit
adoption	adopted	adopt
allegation	alleged	allege
annoyance	annoyed/annoying	annoy
apology	apologetic	apologise
avoidance	(un)avoidable	avoid
benefit	beneficial	benefit
blood	bleeding/bloody	bleed
care	careful/careless	care
(dis)comfort	(un)comfortable	comfort
comparison	comparable	compare
comprehension	(in)comprehensible	comprehend
conflict	conflicting	conflict
consideration	(in)considerate	consider
contradiction	contradictory	contradict
convenience	(in)convenient	inconvenience
corruption	corrupt	corrupt
defence	(in)defensible	defend
disruption	disruptive	disrupt
disturbance	disturbing	disturb
election	elected	elect
electricity	electric/electrical	electrocute
encouragement	encouraging	encourage
enjoyment	enjoyable	enjoy
envy	envious	envy
experience	(in)experienced	experience
extension	extended/extensive	extend

(*Table 2: continued*)

Noun	Adjective	Verb
forgiveness	(un)forgivable	forgive
(in)frequency	(in)frequent	frequent
glamour	glamorous	glamorise
humiliation	humiliating	humiliate
ignorance	ignorant	ignore
information	informative	inform
imagination	imaginative/imaginary	imagine
injury	(un)injured	injure
memory	memorable	memorise
(dis)obedience	(dis)obedient	(dis)obey
persuasion	persuasive	persuade
prediction	(un)predictable	predict
preference	preferable	prefer
prevention	preventive	prevent
protection	protective	protect
provocation	provocative	provoke
regret	regrettable	regret
relaxation	relaxing/relaxed	relax
reliability	(un)reliable	rely (on)
relief	relieved	relieve
retaliation	retaliatory	retaliate
risk	risky	risk
(in)security	(in)secure	secure
sensitivity	(in)sensitive	sensitise
success	(un)successful	succeed
terror	terrifying/terrific	terrify
variety	varied/various/variable	vary

TABLE 3: Noun + adjective

Noun	Adjective	Noun	Adjective
absenteeism	absent (≠ present)	compatibility	(in)compatible
accident	accidental (≠ deliberate)	(in)competence	(in)competent
(in)accuracy	(in)accurate	conceit	conceited (≠ modest)
agility	agile	conscience	conscientious
allergy	allergic	cruelty	cruel (≠ kind)
ambition	(un)ambitious	custom	customary
anger	angry	dynamism	dynamic
appropriateness	(in)appropriate	(in)efficiency	(in)efficient
arrogance	arrogant	eloquence	eloquent
bravery	brave (≠ cowardly)	face	facial
chaos	chaotic	fairness	(un)fair
clumsiness	clumsy	fitness	(un)fit
compassion	compassionate	(in)flexibility	(in)flexible

(Table 3: continued)

Noun	Adjective	Noun	Adjective
fluency	fluent (≠ hesitant)	obsolescence	obsolete
hazard	hazardous	(im)patience	(im)patient
health	(un)healthy	poverty	poor
height	high/tall	probability	(im)probable
honesty	(dis)honest	(ir)regularity	(ir)regular
hostility	hostile	religion	religious
intuition	intuitive (= instinctive)	reluctance	reluctant (≠ willing)
jealousy	jealous	(ir)responsibility	(ir)responsible
laziness	lazy (≠ hardworking)	ruthlessness	ruthless
loyalty	(dis)loyal	selfishness	(un)selfish
method	methodical	skill	skilful
modesty	modest (≠ conceited)	stress	stressful
mood	moody	subjectivity	subjective
muscle	muscular	suicide	suicidal
neutrality	neutral	vagueness	vague (≠ precise)
noise	noisy	violence	violent
objectivity	objective	willingness	(un)willing

TABLE 4: Noun + verb

Noun	Verb	Noun	Verb
abolition	abolish	installation	install
(dis)agreement	(dis)agree	involvement	involve
alteration	alter	loss	lose
amendment	amend	prescription	prescribe
assessment	assess	reaction	react
attendance	attend	recruitment	recruit
betrayal	betray	reduction	reduce
breakdown	break down	rejection	reject
burial	bury	resignation	resign
cancellation	cancel	revelation	reveal
collision	collide	revision	revise
complaint	complain	scrutiny	scrutinise
cremation	cremate	setback	set back
denial	deny (≠ admit)	signature	sign
deterrent	deter	subsidy	subsidise
discovery	discover	suffering	suffer
dismissal	dismiss	summary	summarise
evaluation	evaluate	swelling	swell
expansion	expand	television	televise
flattery	flatter	temptation	tempt
food	feed	threat	threaten
imposition	impose	transformation	transform
insistence	insist (on)	warning	warning

TABLE 5: Both noun and verb

Noun/Verb	Noun/Verb	Noun/Verb	Noun/Verb
ache	compromise	heat	scream
arrest	contact	hug	shout
assault	cough	hurry	shove
average	cure	iron	smell
balance	cut	jump	sneeze
ban	damage	launch	split
bandage	delay	leak	stink
bank	decline	lie	stir
bark	doubt	lock	strike
bend	drop	mention	support
benefit	escape	pledge	swap
bet	experiment	purchase	tap
bias	fine	queue	wave
bomb	flash	regret	whisper
breed	forecast	rise	whistle
bruise	glance	risk	win
bully	grin	riot	witness
care	growl	sack	worry
cash	guess	scare	

Summary of exercises

Unit	Exercises	Self-study activities
1 Learning	1 Keeping vocabulary records 2 Grammar of vocabulary 3 Activating vocabulary: accidents 4 Different meanings of *leave*: dictionary skills	1 Vocabulary revision strategy 2 Topic grouping: sport 3 Different meanings of common verbs
2 Putting things in order	1 Adjective word order: describing people and clothing 2 Frequency and degree adverbs 3 Position of adverbs 4 Past, present and future words, e.g. *recent, current, forthcoming*	1 Personal learning strategy: keeping vocabulary records 2 Adverbs of manner
3 Character and personality	1 Describing people: nouns and adjectives 2 Adjectives + *make* and *do* 3 Qualities needed for different jobs: interpreters and translators	1 Word building 2 Individual learning task 3 Individual learning task
4 Nouns	1 Countable and uncountable nouns 2 Combining nouns: using -'s or the preposition *of* 3 Using nouns as adjectives, e.g. a *two-hour* delay 4 Compound nouns	1 Countable and uncountable nouns 2 Individual learning task 3 Compound nouns
5 Changes	1 Verbs describing change, e.g. *alter* 2 Changes by the year 2000: contextual guesswork 3 Personal changes: transitive vs. intransitive verbs 4 Modernizing a building: verbs and adjectives	1 'Change' verbs, e.g. *melt, fade* 2 New words in the language 3 Individual learning task
6 Revision and expansion	1 Transitive vs. intransitive verbs 2 Short forms, e.g. *influenza (flu)* 3 Noun combinations 4 Compound words 5 Pronunciation 6 Adjectives: personal qualities, e.g. *dishonest, creative*	7 Dialogue building 8 Describing an accident 9 Synonyms and antonyms 10 Pronunciation 11 'Change' verbs 12 Vocabulary storage and revision

Unit	Exercises	Self-study activities
7 Work	1 Different occupations 2 Causes and effects of stress in the workplace 3 Paraphrasing skills and talking about jobs 4 Verb + noun collocations, e.g. *mark essays, obey orders*	1 Idiomatic expressions 2 Compound words 3 Individual learning task
8 Prepositions and phrases	1 Adjectives/verbs + prepositions 2 Prepositional phrases 3 Verb + object + preposition 4 *At* vs. *on* vs. *in*	1 Prepositional phrases 2 'Dangling' prepositions, e.g. the man I told you *about* 3 Different uses of *by*
9 Going places	1 Airport vocabulary 2 Descriptive adjectives: travel brochures 3 Sailing vocabulary + 'action' verbs, e.g. *collide*	1 Geographical features 2 Individual learning task 3 Compound words and common collocations, e.g. *sandy beach*
10 Affixation	1 Adjective suffixes, e.g. *-ate* 2 Verb prefixes, e.g. *mis-* 3 Adjectives often confused, e.g. *economic* vs. *economical*	1 Words with prefix *un-* and suffix *-able* 2 Noun suffix *-ion* 3 Individual learning task
11 Is it right?	1 Objective and subjective words e.g. *balanced, biased* 2 Crime vocabulary 3 Children and the law vocabulary, e.g. *adopt, custody, legal battle*	1 Common mistakes 2 Individual learning task 3 Collocating verbs, e.g. *provoke* and *retaliate*
12 Revision and expansion	1 Verb + noun collocations 2 Organizing vocabulary: hospital, school and prison 3 Odd man out 4 Adjectives/verbs + prepositions 5 Pronunciation: word stress 6 Vocabulary network: travel	7 Quiz on units 7–11 8 Extended writing 9 Prefixes and suffixes 10 Prepositional phrases 11 Occupations 12 Vocabulary revision strategy
13 Newspapers	1 Newspapers in Britain: qualifying vocabulary, e.g. *tend to; to a certain extent* 2 Headline vocabulary: textual synonymy and paraphrase 3 Industrial relations: contextual guesswork	1 Personal learning strategy 2 Headline vocabulary 3 Typographical errors

Unit	Exercises	Self-study activities
14 Verbs	1 Regular and irregular verbs 2 Verb patterns 3 Verb phrases, e.g. *leave me alone* 4 Literal and figurative meanings of common verbs, e.g. *jump, crawl*	1 Irregular verbs 2 Ditransitive verbs 3 Different meanings of *see*: dictionary skills
15 Choices	1 Expressing preferences 2 Household vocabulary 3 Transport vocabulary: focus on *get* and *take*	1 Adjective + noun collocation: household vocabulary 2 Choosing a car 3 Personal learning strategy
16 Connecting words and ideas	1 Link words, e.g. *although* 2 Sentence adverbs, e.g. *apparently* 3 Nouns: examples of a type, e.g. *hammer, saw, screwdriver* are all types of *tool* 4 Text binding vocabulary, e.g. *aspect, issue, rate*	1 Individual learning task 2 Link words and phrases, e.g. *needless to say* 3 Individual learning task
17 Technology	1 Instruments and devices: defining and paraphrasing 2 Expressing the functions of gadgets 3 Describing problems with machines 4 Describing noises, e.g. *buzz, hum*	1 Compounds and collocations, e.g. *floppy disc* 2 Individual learning task 3 Personal learning strategy
18 Revision and expansion	1 Textual synonymy 2 Compound words 3 Household vocabulary 4 Link words 5 Pronunciation: /ə/ and word stress 6 Industrial relations: contextual guesswork	7 Different uses of common verbs 8 Contextual guesswork 9 Defining and paraphrasing 10 Verb patterns 11 Quiz: superordinates, e.g. *insects, tools, facilities* 12 Pronunciation game
19 Customs	1 Cross-cultural behaviour: describing customs/behaviour 2 Weddings and funerals 3 Food and cooking	1 Fixed phrases, e.g. *bless you* 2 Individual learning task 3 Important dates in Britain, e.g. *Boxing Day*
20 Multi-word units	1 Strategies for learning new words in written text 2 Phrasal verbs 3 Different meanings of phrasal verbs: dictionary skills 4 Idiomatic expressions	1 Prepositional phrases (some idiomatic), e.g. *for good* 2 Collocation, e.g. *bored stiff* 3 Personal learning strategy

Unit	Exercises	Self-study activities
21 Men and women	1 Expressing similarities and differences, e.g. *unlike, in common* 2 Job interviews: common phrases and collocations 3 Making connections between words: lexical sets 4 Describing physical and behavioural characteristics of men and women	1 Masculine and feminine words, e.g. *nephew/niece* 2 Individual learning task
22 Ways of saying things	1 Making requests: informal and direct vs. polite and tentative 2 Colloquial vocabulary 3 Expressing positive and negative reactions: connotation 4 Poem: simile and metaphor	1 Common similes in English, e.g. *blind as a bat* 2 Proverbs in English, e.g. *practice makes perfect* 3 Literal and idiomatic meanings of words
23 Ideas and opinions	1 Discussing ideas, e.g. *propose, reject, evaluate* 2 Giving opinions, e.g. *I'm against X, I'm in favour of Y* 3 Media advertising: word building	1 Word building 2 Compound adjectives 3 Keeping vocabulary records
24 Revision and expansion	1 Verbs, e.g. *giggle, stare* 2 Functional dialogues 3 Synonyms: formal vs. informal 4 Talking about national customs 5 Pronunciation: sound and spelling 6 Building lexical sets 7 Similarities and differences 8 Verb + noun collocations	9 Pronunciation: syllables 10 Extreme adjectives 11 Different meanings of words 12 Word building 13 Extended writing 14 Phrases with *get* 15 Antonyms 16 Vocabulary network: food and cooking

A sound way to relieve pain

The Intrason Transducer soothes tired muscles and joints using oscillating sound waves that penetrate to a depth of $2\frac{1}{2}''$ below the skin's surface. Many users of the Intrason Transducer have testified to the pain-killing properties of these sound pulses and have found it an effective alternative to drugs when suffering from rheumatic pains, sciatica, migraine and the aches caused by muscle stress and sports injuries. 240 volts AC only.

One touch monitors your blood pressure

These days more and more of us are taking our blood pressure at home as a way of keeping a regular check on our health. This new portable model from Healthcheck is one of the neatest around, allowing you to take a reading from just the touch of a finger – no more cumbersome arm-bands! The secret is in the totally dependable Pulsonic technology which will give you a reading of both pulse rate and blood pressure on Healthcheck's easy to read digital screen. Fully illustrated, easy to follow instructions are included and Healthcheck comes in an attractive carrying case which takes up very little room when not in use. (1 x AA battery not included).

The ashtray that actually freshens the air

For non-smokers who have to share a house or office with a smoker, this clever new ashtray is great news. It actually draws the smoke down through a special filter and charcoal particles which absorb the smoke and smell, leaving the air around it fresh and clean.
No longer do you have to suffer the discomfort of stuffy rooms where the stale cigarette smoke can hang around for hours. Battery powered, using 2 x C type batteries (not supplied), the ashtray's smart black design means it won't look out of place anywhere.

The portable telephone amplifier

If you're a little hard of hearing or find you often get bad connections or background noise when you're on the phone, this could be the answer. It's a neat battery-operated telephone amplifier which boosts the sound and simply attaches to the earpiece of any telephone using its robust rubber strap. It's easily portable – as it measures just $2\frac{1}{2}'' \times 2\frac{1}{2}'' \times 1''$ it can even go in your pocket – so is also invaluable when staying away from home or for use at a public call box. It is simple to operate using just an on/off switch and a volume control, and comes complete with one AA battery.